CATCHING UP

ISBN: 151537615X
ISBN-13: 978-1515376156

CATCHING UP

Connecting With
Great 21ˢᵗ Century Music

JIM FUSILLI

Contents

INTRODUCTION

A few years ago, it occurred to me that the music industry had little regard for grownups. It chose to ignore us when marketing new music and emerging musicians. Instead, for the most part they fed us reissues of long-ago albums with one, two or more tracks previously considered unworthy of public display. It was as if industry executives believed we were incapable of appreciating any music that was created after, or associated with, our high school or college years.

In some cases, they were correct. There were grownups who weren't worth marketing to. These people tended to respond with bitter intolerance whenever I'd try to engage them in discussions of new bands and recordings. They were dismissive of music they hadn't heard or spent time with, and aggressive in their endorsement of rock and pop from decades ago. They were a minority, to be sure, among music fans of a certain age, but in numbers enough to suggest a trend.

It wasn't much fun to engage in conversation with them. Obtuse and offensive, they were easy to dismantle because they were so obviously wrong. But I began to realize there were ramifications to their positions: it was possible that some reasonable people might believe they knew what they were talking about — because the industry hadn't made the effort to prove them wrong. The idea that good people were being dissuaded from trying new music troubled me.

My January 5, 2012, column for The Wall Street Journal, the publication for which I have been writing about rock and pop since 1983, was entitled "Meet the Gee Bees" — my code for the generationally biased. The article caused quite a stir and some of the reader comments suggested that I had cut too close to the bone. Their anger, disproportionate for anyone but the guilty, told me I might be onto something.

I decided to respond by putting my trust in people who are the opposite of Gee Bees—that is, secure in their status and welcoming of new ideas. Because the industry was ignoring them, what they needed was information. They needed to know that they would find delight in much of the new music that was passing them by. If they were invited to participate, they could root around and make up their own minds.

I deduced that the easiest thing to do was to create a website that introduced a steady diet of new music to grownups. I called it ReNewMusic.net, as in Re. New Music and ReNew Music. The tagline: Music for Grownups. ReNewMusic. net extended an open invitation to anyone who was willing to accept it. Soon enough, visitors would know whether they belonged.

One ReNewMusic.net feature that proved popular was "Catching Up," a weekly series that examined great 21st-century albums and what makes them special. The capsule reviews endeavor to introduce artists and their albums to music fans who may know little or nothing about them. In some cases, the artists are household names (though perhaps not for their music) and others are fairly obscure. In each case, I felt they had made albums worthy of grownup music fans' time and attention.

As the "Catching Up" reviews began to mount, I noticed that they seemed to take on a different meaning when read in a flurry, rather than once per week. They provided a kind of a report on the state of popular music. I thought it might be a good idea to provide people curious about new music and today's music scene with a portable, easy-to-access guide.

*　　*　　*

So now we have this book, which collects the first 50 "Catching Up" reviews — 50 reviews of albums released in the past 15 years that I think you might find somewhere between interesting and fantastic. The verdict on each, and the music scene as a whole, is entirely up to you.

In reading the reviews — and, far more importantly — listening to the recordings, I believe you will hear what has been evident to me for a while now: great songs are still being written; great singers are still moving us with their voices and expressiveness; great musicians are still playing with innovation and feeling; and great arrangers are still finding the best ways to shape music so it can touch us at the core. In this new music, some based on long-standing traditions, others with sounds that come at us as if born before our ears and eyes, we hear the musicians' supreme desire to communicate to us, regardless of our age and station in life. Through their music, they welcome us to a world we may have forgotten we share.

Sometimes that world is a bit hard to fathom. Much has changed. The old radio stations are gone. So is the local record shop. Rock magazines morphed a while ago into lifestyle publications, and new music blogs sprout like weeds. For many among us, it's challenge to figure out where to turn and how to re-engage.

My series of essays entitled "How To Enjoy New Music" tries to smooth the re-entry. In some cases, all that's required to step back in is a sense of adventure and a tweak to attitude. There are new radio stations, new places to acquire music; good music journalism can be found. It's easy to adapt — if you want to adapt. I suspect that, if you're interested in catching up, the new world won't provide much of an obstacle. If you're a grownup, you've beaten back bigger challenges. There's no reason to think you won't succeed once again.

New music needs us, and I believe we need new music too. I wish you much happiness in your quest for it and deep satisfaction once you find it. I hope it brings brings you the great joy you've earned and deserve.

Chelsea Wolfe

HOW TO ENJOY NEW MUSIC

Brittany Howard and Zac Cockrell of Alabama Shakes

BOBBY TALAMINE

Ignore the Gee Bees!
Rock & Pop Is As Great
As It's Ever Been

The biggest obstacle to grownups enjoying new music may be the tyranny of generational orthodoxy — which is a fancy way of saying we're surrounded by people who, despite a narrow perspective, insist the music of their youth is superior to the sounds of any other period.

The ready availability of new recorded music as well as albums and tracks from the '30s, '40s and so on has reduced the tyrant to a crazy man at the side of the road, shaking his fist at the rush toward modernity and beyond. But for some among us, the view of today's rock and pop scene is still shaped by biases that have taken tumor-like root. Most people who prefer old music mean no harm and it's often a pleasure to listen to them talk about their favorite artists of the distant past. But others are bullies who intend to harangue us into submission, as if their bluster can conceal their ignorance. They ignore what seems to me something that's self-evident: rock and pop today is as good as it's ever been.

Popular music has had some remarkable periods and remarkable years. In 1991, about a quarter-century ago now, "Use Your Illusions I & II" by Guns N' Roses, "Loveless" by My Bloody Valentine, "Nevermind" by Nirvana, "Ten" by Pearl Jam, "Screamadelica" by Primal Scream," "Out of Time" by R.E.M. and "The Low End Theory" by A Tribe Called Quest were among the new albums.

If we step away from rock and pop for a moment, we see that 1959 was almost miraculous: "Time Out" by the Dave Brubeck Quartet, "The Genius of Ray Charles," "The Shape of Jazz to Come" by Ornette Coleman," "Giant Steps" by John Coltrane, "Kind of Blue" by Miles Davis, "Ella Fitzgerald Sings the George and Ira Gershwin Songbook," "Satan is Real" by the Louvin Brothers, and "Mingus Ah Um" by Charles Mingus all were released during that year.

But you can be sure that '59 and '91 had their share of stinkers too: mediocre albums, pandering albums, dumb albums, trendy albums, copycat albums and so on and so forth. Even in the best periods, great and ground-breaking recordings are a minority. In general, when someone with a generational bias — heretofore known as a Gee Bee — starts listing a certain period's great albums as evidence of its superiority to today's music, your rebuttal could be to list all the crummy albums that were released in the same period. Your list will be longer by a geometric amount.

To be fair, there's the argument that today's music is worse than yesteryear's simply because digital recording, home studios and distribution via the web have encouraged more people of questionable talent to make tracks. But access to recording technology also allows talented people to develop their musical skills. Mark Mothersbaugh of Devo once told me he thought the ratio of good-to-bad recorded music today was the same as it ever was, and that makes sense to me.

Remember the crazy man at the side of the road who insists on telling us how much greater music used to be? You will find that people like him often lack the fundamental capacity to tell good from bad. If they listen to new music at all, their judgment is clouded not only by generational bias, but also by the detritus of the recording industry's powerful marketing machinery. They may know trivia, history, sales figures, popularity and the level of influence on the culture or fashion of a certain artist, all of which may make them formidable candidates for "Jeopardy!" But they know nothing about music, which, to quote Wiki, is the "art form whose medium is sound. Its common elements are pitch, which governs melody and harmony, rhythm…dynamics and the sonic qualities of timbre and texture." Here's a useful rule of thumb: when someone who knows nothing about music insists an old album is great and a new one isn't, ask him how he can tell.

I believe most of us who keep an open mind about new music can know what's good through experience and a form of intuition. I mean, nobody has to tell us that Adele or Richard Hawley can sing, that Laura Marling or Lorde can turn a phrase, that Gary Clark Jr. or Kenneth Pattengale can play the guitar, or that Chris Thile can play the mandolin. We can rightfully claim they are good, even if our only explanation is that we've been listening to new music steadily for long enough to trust our ability to recognize quality. Because we ignore the crazy man at the side of the road, we can appreciate great music from any era.

It's Not Your Fault: Media Culpability in the Bias Against New Music

Now that we're ready to disarm any Gee Bee who insists rock and pop music was better when he was a kid, we're faced with another challenge: what to do about bias in media?

We know that a knee-jerk prejudice against media is a sign of a dull mind. But truth is, there are media outlets, music critics and entertainment reporters in the guise of critics who are Gee Bees too. In some cases, they conceal it well, at least at first blush.

Take, as an example, Rolling Stone magazine, in particular its "Best Of" lists. Back when it was launched about a half-century ago, Rolling Stone was considered a definitive source of knowledgeable commentary on rock and pop. But it's been forever since Cameron Crowe, Ben Fong-Torres, Ralph Gleason and Jon Landau were writing for it, and though David Fricke is as hardworking a reporter as you'll find in the field, Rolling Stone isn't a magazine primarily interested in great, innovative music.

It leverages its former reputation on occasion with special editions designed to appeal to music fans who remember its glory days. Good business that may be, but by doing so, Rolling Stone stokes the fire under Gee Bees, who, having been shaped to a degree by the magazine's opinions three or four decades ago, may fail to see its "Best Of" publications as a circulation grab.

Take a look at one of its recent 500 Greatest Albums of All Time issues. Only one album in its top 10 was released after 1979: "London Calling" by the Clash, which appeared in the U.S. in January 1980. Of the 500 albums on the list, 292 — a whopping 59 percent — were released in the '60s or '70s. Only eight percent were released in this century; only two were issued this decade, including "Smile" by the Beach Boys, which was recorded 48 years ago. Kanye West's "My Beautiful Dark Twisted Fantasy" is ranked 353rd, surrounded by albums by the Yardbirds. It doesn't take much to see that a list that includes four albums by the Beatles, two by Bob Dylan and one each by the Beach Boys, the Rolling Stones and Marvin Gaye in its top 10 is designed to appeal to boomers. Open-minded music fans see it for what it is, but for the generationally biased among us, it's fuel or, worse, fact.

But Rolling Stone isn't only publication that's guilty of generational bias. Pitchfork, the web-based publication that launched in 1995, aims special reports at its base. In late 2009, it published its staff's picks for Best Albums of the 2000s. Only one album recorded by an artist who began his career in the '60s or '70s appeared among the top 200: "Abattoir Blues/Lyre of Orpheus" by Nick Cave and his band the Bad Seeds. (Cave's first album, with the Boys Next Door, came out in '79.) The list omitted Brian Wilson's rendition of "Smile," the Blind Boys of Alabama's "Spirit of the Century," Robert Plant and Alison Krauss's "Raising Sand," Raphael Saadiq's "The Way I See It," Ray Wylie Hubbard's "Enlightenment," Leonard Cohen and Sharon Robinson's "Ten New Songs," and Cave's superior "Dig Lazarus Dig!!!" among others. To be fair, amidst the snarkiness that's characteristic of Pitchfork, the capsule reviews cite '60s and '70s artists as influences, and its top 10, led by Radiohead's "Kid A," seemed just about right.

Thus, when it comes to music publications, it's always wise to consider for a moment to whom they seek to appeal before giving credence to their opinions.

Sometimes, it's not so much the publication, but the critic who reveals a bias. If a journalist is transparent about it, that's fine: most people who endeavor to earn a living writing about rock and pop do so because we love music; on occasion we get excited and forget that what we like isn't necessary up to the critical standards we would apply to an unfamiliar artist. But if the bias crops up consistently and without explanation, it can be damaging — to readers and to new musicians. As readers, we need to be on guard: if we've been reading someone for decades, we may not realize that he hasn't adapted to changes in how music is made and how what's new deserves the same respect as what's familiar. He may have helped dig the rut we're stuck in. At the same time, though, we know intuitively if he's open to the new — because he's pulled us forward with him. More often than not, the writing is expression of the joy of discovery, and neither defensive nor self-protective.

Imagine if in 1963, a critic with a bias for swing music had knocked "The Freewheelin' Bob Dylan" for its lack of clarinet solos. As silly as that seems, something similar happens today when a veteran critic refuses to acknowledge, or even investigate, the value of what's new. He may prefer Max Roach vs. a complex synthesized drum track, but that doesn't mean synthesized percussion isn't valid. The open-minded critic evaluates the relatively new form not against Roach, but whether it serves its function. He doesn't dismiss new technologies because he doesn't approve. I love Roach's work, but the percussion on dZihan & Kamien's "Stiff Jazz" delights me too. No one with a beating heart can claim the latter doesn't swing — unless, as policy, he rejects the new approach. By the way, the reverse is true as well: don't listen to a tuba in a New Orleans-style brass band and compare it what Bernie Worrell achieves on a bass synth. It's not fair to anyone, no one more so than readers.

We hear from some quarters that the standard for rock and pop criticism isn't what it once was. That may be so, given that anyone can open a blog and call himself a critic. But a critic must know music — again, "pitch, which governs melody and harmony, rhythm...dynamics and the sonic qualities of timbre and texture." If you come upon a journalist who claims he's a critic but doesn't know music, he's not a critic.

At the same time, though, the standard used by some Gee Bees to evaluate today's professional critics — writers whose opinions must stand the rigors of the editorial process — is often a fantasy of what once was. Not every critic of yesteryear dispensed wisdom and insight. If you've had a chance to read newspapers and magazines from the '40s, you discovered that all sorts of journalists, particularly gossip columnists, opined on music when it's obvious they knew nothing more than what a publicist told them. Not everyone who wrote for Rolling Stone was Crowe, Fong-Torres, Gleason or Landau. Absent proof, to suggest then was better than now may be to indulge in a bias.

In short, yes, media can be culpable in compelling us to look back while dismissing what's now and what's ahead, and can be just as unfair to new music, musicians and the music-making process as the biased music fan. But there are talented, open-minded critics eager to share the joys of new music while respecting what came before. It's our choice whether to trust or disregard writers and publications that deal in bias.

Today, the Gatekeeper Is You

f memory serves, finding out about new music once went something like this: we heard a single on AM radio, we went to the local record shop and we bought it. Or we heard a track on FM radio, we went to the local record shop and we bought the album. Or we saw a video on MTV, we went to the local record shop and we bought the single or the album. Somewhere along the line, we may have checked with our favorite music magazine to see if it endorsed an album we were thinking of buying.

The entire process was governed by the recording industry.

Today, very few gatekeepers stand between new music and us. And it may be the artists themselves who notify us that their new music is on its way.

Ah, the wonders of disintermediation.

For those of us who were raised with the recording industry perched on our shoulders, it can be a bit difficult to adjust to such freedom. Musty old habits claw at us from the grave. But the fact is that in many cases we can hear the music before or at about the same time the gatekeepers announce their opinions. Each week, NPR Music and other public radio stations premiere several new albums well in advance of release. Rock blogs launch new tracks. Mainstream media is in the game too.

Each Friday, Spotify posts for streaming most of the week's new albums. If streaming services aren't to your liking, vendors like iTunes and Amazon offer a taste of tracks from new releases; iTunes has unique content on occasion. Videos released by bands in anticipation of their albums' street dates are up on YouTube. Best of all, artists place a lot of new music on their websites; fans who sign up for mailing lists get a shot of all sorts of new music before the rest of us.

Yes, there's a subtle form of pre-approval at work here — to my

BOBBY TALAMINE

Kevin Parker of Tame Impala

knowledge, NPR Music doesn't premiere albums it thinks are awful and rock blogs have a tendency to tout music by the kind of music their readers like. Visitors to deathmetal.org and newagemusic.com have certain expectations, after all. The recording industry still promotes to, and aims advertising at, grownups, though not with the frequency and intensity that it does to younger and, one assumes, more impressionable listeners.

For the most part, we can access new music without filters, without gatekeepers, without social pressure. All we have to do is listen — and finding new music to listen to is a snap. Isn't it terrifically liberating to have a chance to make up our own minds?

The More You Listen,
The More You Know

One sunny afternoon not long ago, my wife and I decided to cool down with a drink. The bar was near empty but, as bad luck would have it, in attendance was a certified Gee Bee, his generational bias about music as apparent as the mousse in his thinning gray hair. "There are no singer-songwriters anymore," he said, loud enough for all to hear. "Today, they don't even write their own music."

The wound from biting my knuckle will heal soon.

The problem with the Gee Bee in the bar is apparent: he does not listen so he does not know. He does not know so thoroughly, so absolutely, that he doesn't know how much he doesn't know. Every bar has its share of gasbags oblivious to their ignorance, and as my wife pointed out, even his date seemed bored by his bloviation. But you know as well as I do that his opinion is shared by other Gee Bees among us. And if you love music, you know it's a particularly venomous form of yammering — because there are impressionable people who might believe what he says is true.

As Gee Bees are wont to do, he presented his opinion as fact, unaware how easily it is to disprove. Singer-songwriters are abundant today, as anyone who follows popular music beyond the hit-seeking mainstream knows. Folk music is everywhere in the truest sense of the word — we can listen to recordings of original compositions by contemporary folk artists from all over the planet. Here at home, the Americana movement is predicated on singers who write their songs. Countless rock bands perform songs written by one of their members who could sit down and play it solo if he chose to, as many R&B artists can with their compositions.

When we listen to these contemporary singer-songwriters we are assured that the tradition is in great hands; that is, there are as many terrific singer-songwriters today as at any time in rock and pop's rich history. Whether

BOBBY TALAMINE

Tunde Adebimpe of TV on the Radio

they will have careers as lengthy and fruitful as some of their predecessors isn't yet apparent; that is to say, it's too early to know whether today's best singer-songwriters be held in consistent high esteem as is Leonard Cohen or be as forgotten as David Ackles. Or who among them will see a revival like that of Nick Drake, who was hardly a presence in the '80s and '90s, but is beloved once again today almost 40 years after his death. Perhaps the new singer-composers will have careers as versatile and brilliant as Paul Simon, who's made some of his best music in the latter stages of his career. It's too soon to tell.

But time, and what's occurs in its passage, means nothing to the likes of the Gee Bee at the end of the bar. Fair play isn't his concern. He'd rather dismiss the work of extraordinary artists than to check to see if his opinions are valid. He does not listen so he does not know.

We may have to suffer Gee Bees on occasion, but in the end it is they who lose. Because, unlike those of us who listen and know, they will never be aware of the joy and wonder of what they have not heard.

The Reminiscence Bump

P sychologists say grownups have a tendency to recollect more, and with greater clarity, events that occurred in adolescence and early adulthood than during any other period in our lives. This phenomenon is described as the "reminiscence bump." Studies also have shown that grownups recall and recognize the music of their late teens and early twenties with greater specificity and stronger emotions than music from other periods.

I haven't found anyone for whom this isn't true.

It's sweet and satisfying that there's music that's traveled within us into our adult years, don't you agree? But there's a danger in misunderstanding what the reminiscence bump means. I'm certain there are among us Gee Bees — the generationally biased — who believe the reminiscence bump has something to do with the music's quality rather than the period in which it was first heard and appreciated. No psychologist or layman, as far as I can tell, has proposed that the music of our youth is better than what preceded or followed it just because we can recall it clearly and viscerally.

Nor does the reminiscence bump preclude us from appreciating and enjoying music from other eras.

My WSJ colleague Terry Teachout posted an observation on Facebook: "If you still like all of the music that you liked when you were in high school — and nothing else — you probably don't really like music." I agree completely. The folks to whom Terry refers are fond of something beyond the music of the reminiscence-bump period. They may be caught in the sway of nostalgia or sentiment; that is, the music of their youth means much to them because it was soundtrack to life events they consider seminal. Again, that's sweet. But it has nothing to do with whether old music is better than what's new. As stated earlier, what we like and what's great may be entirely separate.

We often hear grownups talk about the kind of music they enjoyed as teens as if it were a sign of character. And it may have been: you may know the only person in high school who chose, out of a genuine conviction and taste, a favorite band in opposition to what everyone else liked. But it's likely he enjoyed the same music as other members of his tribe. Maybe that's why we joined our tribes: we liked the same music. Or, bonded by other commonalities, we gravitated together to a certain kind of music with which we could identity as a collective. Music was part of our identity.

It's undeniable that the industry and its agents, including FM radio, MTV and the trade press, exploited the concept of music as identity in their marketing strategies. When we bought a T-shirt with our favorite band's name on it, we were announcing something about ourselves and it wasn't based entirely, or even primarily, on the quality of the music. We were saying we belonged to ... whatever it was we belonged to.

But for grownups, that sort of thing really doesn't work, does it? I mean, by a certain age, it's not so great if our identity is built primarily on the kind of bands we like. But we were raised to like, and to declare we like, music with which we can identify. It's a hard habit to break.

But I believe "music as identity" puts us at a distant from young musicians and their music, even if we like it, because we are accustomed to identifying with the image of the artists as much, as if not more so, than with the quality of the music.

Kind of silly, right? As grownups, we can like what we like regardless of what image the artist projects. We know who we are. Our identities are built on substantive matters: family, friends, achievement, service, faith and so forth. Liberated from having to identify with musicians' images, we are free to like music as music — not as soundtrack, as it was decades and scores ago, to some idealized version of who we think we are or would like to be. And we can enjoy today's music without discarding the best music of our youth: there's room in us for music from all eras.

The New
Reframes the Familiar

O ne of the joys of listening to new music is it changes the way we listen to old music.

New music encourages us to listen differently. Musical concepts we may have thought minor or disinteresting may appeal to today's musician who push them to the fore, thus all but challenging us to reassess our opinions. They've giving us a gift, if you think about it: learning something new that causes us to change our minds is one of the joys of growing older. Few things are as refreshing.

Back in the 1970s and '80s, I wasn't a disco fan, though I did like the R&B touches in the hits. But some of the electronic and dance music I like today has disco at its roots — as Daft Punk pointed out in their lengthy track "Giorgio by Moroder" on their '13 album "Random Access Memories." (Moroder is best known for co-producing Donna Summer's biggest hits.) We also hear disco's influence in big pop singles by Bruno Mars, Katy Perry, Robin Thicke, Pharrell Williams and other chart-minded artists, as well as in acts like Arcade Fire (on "Reflektor"), !!!, Planningtorock, Todd Terje and others. If we enjoy any of those artists, it's a small step to revisit '70s disco. With new ears, we hear the tight arrangements seamlessly executed under brassy, soulful vocals we may have missed decades ago. As an experiment, try "Got to Be Real" by Cheryl Lynn, "Love Thang" by First Choice, "Double Exposure" by Ten Percent or any number of tracks by Chic or MFSB. If you've been listening to new music, you may discover that the classic disco tracks sound different now than they did back then. Of course, they haven't changed. But we have.

Remixes have altered my appreciation for some old tracks, or at least altered my perception on why they're so good. Check out DJ Smash's remix of Stevie Wonder's "Signed, Sealed, Delivered" (I'm Yours)" on the 2005 album "Motown Remixed." The producer took Wonder's 1970s hit, opened up the backing track and highlighted Mike Terry's baritone sax. It's a terrific reinvention, and I don't believe you can listen to the highly textured original in the same way after hear-

Michael Shurman and Zach Dawes of Mini Mansions

ing what DJ Smash loved about it. Similarly, the Ummah remix of Grant Green's "Down Here on the Ground," on 1996's "The New Groove: The Blue Note Remix Project" album, highlights elements of the track we may have overlooked.

Another approach to revisiting old music is through appreciating who is influencing today's musicians. Back in the late '90s, Beth Orton spoke to me of her admiration for Terry Callier, who made six albums in the '60s and '70s. I listened to his music, which I bypassed completely decades earlier, and found it rich and intriguing. In the past two or so years, there's been a revival of psychedelic pop music that references an era that occurred about 20 years before contemporary musicians like Jacco Gardner, Ariel Pink and Darwin Smith were born. While listening to the new sunny music, I revisited the Association and dusted off the "Nuggets From Nuggets: Choice Artyfacts From The First Psychedelic Era" boxed set to listen to the Count Five, Electric Prunes, the Seeds and so on — bands I hadn't listened to, at least not intentionally, in many, many years.

The point is: if we open our minds and revisit the songs and albums of our past with a fresh viewpoint on what makes music enjoyable, we may find that some of the best new music is actually something we missed or didn't value in the past.

Shazam!

O ne of the ways many of us are introduced to new music is via television. Not only by the likes of "Austin City Limits," "Later... with Jools Holland" and various live-music showcases on AXS TV, Palladia and late-night programs that squeeze in a performance before the credits, but also during dramatic series, which often use contemporary rock and pop recordings to augment the original score.

The problem with music in TV dramas is, almost without exception, the producers fail to tell us what we've heard. We get neither the song nor the artist's name. So, unless we search online in the days after the broadcast, we're left without a way to hear the song again or to find other music by the artist. It's frustrating, particularly if we're excited enough to want to hear the song again and again.

But, as we know, if there's a problem, there's a solution, usually created by those who spot a business opportunity. One way we can find out what recordings we've heard on TV, radio or just about anywhere recorded music is played is by using a smartphone-based music identifications system. Perhaps the best known of these systems is Shazam, which claims some 450 million users.

Shazam is simple to use: download the free app for either Apple or Android operating systems; when you hear a recording you can't place, quickly activate the app and then tap the smartphone screen (takes less than 10 seconds); Shazam will listen for a identifying code that's been embedded in the recording; and will send you the name of the song and the artist as well as a link to where you can purchase the recording. For some films and TV shows, the app will identify at once every track in the program. Also, in many cases, Shazam will let you listen to the song via Rdio or Spotify, immediately or later. Now and then, Shazam also scrolls the song's lyrics. And it will link you to an online vendor so you can purchase the song or the album from which it's culled.

The app saves what it calls tags, and I have a database of about 130 songs I had the urge to discover or, in some cases due to faulty memory, rediscover. For example, my tag list tells me I didn't recognize "Long Hard Time" by Gangstagrass in a January 29, 2013, episode of "Justified." I'd never heard before "Indita MIA" by the APM Latin Players that appeared in "Ray Donovan." In 2014, I Shazamed a song by the Monkees I'm sure I hadn't heard in more than 40 years (and would be happy to ignore for the next 40). It works for commercials too: Shazam is how I learned Miike Snow's "Paddling Out" was the song in an annoying beer commercial. A tag list of 130 songs indicates I've used the system quite often — and I like to think I'm up on all sorts of different recordings from different eras. It's a valuable aid and it can be a lot of fun.

If I'm at a club and don't know what the DJ is spinning, I'll Shazam chunks of his set — I did so at Terminal 5 in New York a while ago when Flume mixed in tunes I didn't know and few weeks earlier at a Maya Jane Coles show at the Public Works in San Francisco. I've Shazamed the music blasting over the P.A. before a band goes onstage, and I've Shazamed in restaurants and clothing stores and near hidden speakers in malls. Perhaps I'm confessing to a moving violation here, but I've Shazamed the car radio while driving — usually for an obscure instrumental track KCRW spun while the DJ spoke. You know the feeling: when we hear music we like, we want to know more about it.

I'm not endorsing Shazam. It's far from the only music-identification service. Soundhound, Musixmatch and MusicID are worth exploring. Facebook and Google have music-identification features. Shazam has a premium service, but I've never found a need to upgrade. There may be other such services.

I doubt their manufacturers thought their products would be memory aids for grownup rock fans, but I find in many cases when I look at the list of tags, I can recall where I was when I searched for the name of the track. I was sitting in the Blu Jam Café in West Hollywood when the Bud Shank Quintet's "Jasmine" came on and in a Popeye's in Harlem when a Carlos Santana-Fher Olvera track burst from the speakers. During a short stay at a hotel in Memphis in September 2012, I sought the names of tracks by the Astors, Walter Jackson, Jackie Moore and Peggy Scott — believe it or not, I heard every one of those cuts while riding up or down in an elevator. That's how quickly a music-identification can work, and it doesn't matter if the music is old, brand new or somewhere in between. If you want to know what it is, you can find out in seconds without difficulty.

Live and In Concert

B ack in the old days, bands would tour in order to sell albums. Today, bands release albums in order to stir interest in their tours.

OK. That last line is a bit hyperbolic. Bands make albums for many reasons, not the least of which are to express emotion and perspective, and to capture their development as artists. But a new recording is often the springboard for touring. These days, most bands earn their living, such as it is, on the road.

The shift in focus to live performance influences how we enjoy new music and support working musicians. It's to our benefit — but only if we go to shows.

It can be risky, as well as expensive, to take a chance on a night out for music, though I'd argue not as risky as it once was. Today's musicians have to play well live or they can't sustain a career, so the odds are in your favor that you'll get a good show from an act you've sampled via radio, TV, YouTube or a streaming service. Bands tour relentless nowadays so it may be likely they'll come somewhere near where you live, especially if a sizable college is nearby.

But even the most ardent new music fans among grownups can't be expected to go to four or five shows a week or even a month. So how to see all those bands —new ones as well as veterans who are doing great new work — that have perked your interest?

At a festival, where you'll have an opportunity to see many bands for what amounts to a bargain price per act.

If you're envisioning a miserable time in the muck, chomping on dirty-water hot dogs and peeing in the woods, know that long gone are the days when a rock festival was a free-for-all with few amenities and little personal security. The ones I attend are as well run as any stadium or arena show. Many forms of transportation are available; food is bountiful and generally above the quality served at sports events; there are rows of portable toilets and water to wash and stay fresh; and the sound is better than you could imagine. I can't think of

CHRIS MILLER

Coachella

the last time I went to a festival that I didn't think was worthwhile.

From spring through fall, festivals all across the U.S. and Canada present superior talent on multiple stages. The big-name events get the most buzz — Ultra in Miami in March; Coachella in Indio, California, in April; Bonnaroo in Manchester, Tennessee, in June; Lollapalooza in Chicago in August, to name a few — but they are far from the only major ones. Festivals with diverse lineups include the Hangout Festival in Gulf Shores, Alabama, in May; Sasquatch! in George, Washington, also in May; in June, Governors Ball in New York City and the Firefly Music Festival in Dover, Delaware; Pitchfork Music Festival in Chicago in July; and Austin City Limits Festival in October. There are many, many others across the U.S. and Canada.

I see more and more men and women in their 40s, 50s and 60s at today's rock festivals. (They may be in their 70s for all I know.) There's usually a lot of walking involved and a 12-hour day can seem much longer if the music sags or the sun's bearing down, but there are places to refresh and recharge. I've never witnessed a grownup being made to feel unwelcomed by young fans at a rock festival. I'm guessing once you decide to make festivals part of your new-music mix, you'll be glad you did.

Go. Listen. Celebrate!

n the ReNew Music series "How to Enjoy New Music," we've tried to make it easier to find and enjoy the artistry of today's rock-and-pop musicians who are comparable to those at any time in the history of popular music.

Much of what the series says can be boiled down to: if you enjoyed rock and pop years ago, there are no restrictions to doing so now. Don't let Gee Bees — the generationally biased, that is — persuade you that popular music was better way back when. As discussed in early chapters, the power of the recording industry back in the '70s created a sense of superiority in a certain type of rock-music fan — closed mind and tyrannical, to be kind. But the ready availability of new recorded music as well as albums and tracks from the '30s, '40s and so on has reduced the tyrant to a crazy man at the side of the road. We know that there's been great music in every period since recorded music began.

If you find yourself engaged with a Gee Bee in a conversation about music, you can extricate yourself quickly by asking him a simple question: how do you know the music of your youth is better than what we have today? If you stay around to hear the answer, it will reveal the flaw in his position. If he doesn't know music — and I don't mean trivia, history, sales figures, popularity or influence on the culture or fashion — his opinion is likely to be without foundation. ("Likely to be" because some independent-minded musician may have told him what's good.) Also, it's seems a common trait among Gee Bees that they will opine on new music without listening to it. If someone doesn't listen, he can't know. Full stop.

It's an good idea to be aware that some media feed the biases not only of Gee Bees but all of us who aren't on guard. Rolling Stone, for example, leverages its former reputation with special "Best Of" editions designed to appeal to music fans who remember its glory days decades ago. Pitchfork, the web-based publication that launched in 1995, aims special reports at its Gen-X base.

Sometimes, the bias isn't in the publication, but in a particular journalist.

If his bias crops up consistently and without explanation, it can be damaging — to readers and to new musicians. If you feel a journalist isn't open to new sounds, drop him from your list of advisers. He's out to hurt you. Much like a radio station that plays only a certain stream of classic rock, he wants to lock you into a world that acknowledges only his biased point of view.

Music fans can bypass the opinion of critics and discover new music on our own. We have access now to new music before it's on sale and before critics chirp about it. NPR Music premieres albums regularly well in advance of release. Platforms like iTunes offer previews of tracks from forthcoming discs. Each week, streaming services like Spotify post new albums the day they're available to consumers. The music fan is the gatekeeper now and I think we're all the better for it.

Because I'm so bullish on new music and today's musicians, Gee Bees and other grumps accuse me of hating old music. It's a lame tactic. I'm bullish on old music too — not all of it; and I don't confuse sentiment with good taste. I think those of us who've been listening to new music for decades straight through to now are blessed. We know the history and we can hear the influences. It's a great platform for discussion with young music fans who, I find, are open to music from any era.

Those young, open-minded fans contribute to the joy of attending rock festivals, which I think are the best way to discover new music in abundance. I've yet to feel unwelcomed or out of place at a festival where the average age of the audience is about 30 — that is, half my age. Someone did something right in raising these kids in the world of music. I wish I had been as open-minded when I was their age.

Most rock musicians earn their keep these days by performing, be it in a tiny, sweaty club or in a tent at a major festival. I don't want to suggest it's our duty to support their endeavors, but if you enjoy new music and the adventure of exploring for it, going to shows profits you and the musicians. As part of my job, I go to shows and it's not always comfortable: overcrowding; bad sightlines; late, late nights; and, as opposed to you who will venture out with friends, I'm often alone. But something happens when the music kicks in. All the issues I might have been grousing about in my mind suddenly disappear, and it's just the music and me. It's an experience that's never lost its wonder for me. If you've been away from the club scene or concert venues, I think if you return to hear live music you might have the kind of transporting experience that I do. I encourage you to get back into it and have a blast. You've earned it.

Ezra Fuhrman

CONNECTING WITH GREAT 21ST CENTURY MUSIC

Mer de Noms

A Perfect Circle | *2000*

Patience
proved
the greatest
virtue for
A Perfect
Circle

From A Perfect Circle's beginning, Maynard James Keenan insisted the band wasn't subservient to his group Tool, a concert headliner and seller of albums by the millions. That's a refrain offered often by musicians who move on, if only for a while, but in Keenan's case it felt true. A Perfect Circle's explosive, unsettling debut, "Mer de Noms," reflected his passion and intensity as a singer and lyricist.

A Perfect Circle had a serendipitous start. Billy Howerdel was a guitar technician for a number of popular alternative bands, including Tool and Nine Inch Nails. In 1995, while crashing at Keenan's home, Howerdel played him a tape of songs he'd written and recorded, handling most instruments himself. They decided to form a partnership. Soon, bassist/violinist Paz Lenchantin, guitarist Troy Van Leeuwen and drummer Tim Alexander joined them. Alexander departed during the recording sessions, replaced by the extraordinary Josh Freese.

Tool was a major influence on "Mer de Noms," and not merely because Keenan was its voice. Tool expanded metal's vocabulary in the mid-1990s, as it evolved to explore a wide range of musical forms. Similarly, A Perfect Circle had its pick from among many approaches to rock and, for the most part, Howerdel chose roar and power as its foundation.

But patience was the greatest virtue of "Mer de Noms": the band let the songs unfold. The ballad "Breña" was built from a single electric guitar, but never completely exploded into chaos; Howerdel's melodic guitar solo guided it to its end. A folk guitar and a tambourine provided unexpected interludes in the growling "Rose," and in the gem "Magdalena," all instruments except the drums dropped out then re-entered with the aural equivalent of a glare and a sneer. In "3 Libras," strings scored by Lenchantin accompanied Keenan on one of his most affecting performances on the disc.

Freese, meanwhile, never overplayed, and his appreciation for space gave the music its airiness without losing its sense of aggression. The simple pattern he played under the intro to "Judith" added texture to the performance and, wisely, he didn't alter it much when Keenan's raging "Cookie Monster" vocal entered with the squealing guitars.

As for Keenan, for the most part he kept down the volume, his voice alternating between shockingly sweet and desperately menacing. And he contributed the ideal lyrics to Howerdel's dark songs, touching on such anguished themes as psychological turmoil and a compulsion for self-destruction and violence. "Judith" was all upheaval and blasphemy; reportedly, the song was about Keenan's reaction to childhood memories of his mother's stroke and its aftermath.

A Perfect Circle went on to record two more studio albums — "Thirteen Steps" issued in 2003; and "eMoTIVe," an '04 set in which 10 of 12 songs were covers — with some changes in personnel. With only Howerdel and Keenan remaining from the original lineup, A Perfect Circle reunited in 2010 for a concert tour that extended into '11 and resulted in several live discs, including one of "Mer de Noms" from top to bottom. Howerdel recorded under the name Ashes Divide, and Keenan now fronts the band Puscifer. Rumors of new music by A Perfect Circle come and go.

On "Mer de Noms," the short-lived version of the quintet made an extraordinary musical statement, one that put rage and patience side by side to produce a surprising and disquieting result.

21

Adele | *2011*

The wounds of her experience informed the recording to give its raw core.

With her rich voice and mature delivery, Adele delivered in 2008 a debut album, "19," that was rooted in gospel, R&B and Motown. It was a hit in most major markets including the U.S., where she won a Grammy as Best New Artist. For "21," the follow-up recording, Adele responded by altering her style. Her superior talent made the transition flawless.

During her 2008-'09 U.S. tour behind "19," the British singer absorbed some country and Americana music, enjoying singers like Wanda Jackson, Alison Krauss, Hillary Scott and Chris Stapleton, among others. As importantly, she came to appreciate the directness and transparency in country and Americana songwriting.

As it turned out, she had much to say on "21": the sessions began as she and her boyfriend were breaking up, and the lyrics reflected her emotional turmoil. The wounds of her experience informed the recording to give its raw core.

With her musical palette expanded, in October 2009 — one day after the breakup — Adele returned to the studio in London where she and Paul Epworth wrote "Rolling in the Deep" in less than 15 minutes. Their demo remained central to the final track, which became a massive worldwide hit. Released in November 2010, about six weeks before the album, it served to represent Adele's new sound. The percussion by Leo Taylor and acoustic guitar by Epworth are Americana, the vibe — as well as handclaps and choir — are soul and gospel. The blend worked beautifully.

Moving ahead, Adele employed several producers on "21." Using his studio in Malibu, Rick Rubin chose to place the singer in an intimate setting with drummer Chris Dave, guitarist Matt Sweeney, the Roots' James Poyser on keyboards and Pino Palladino on bass. Written with Dan Wilson, "Don't You Remember" opened with Adele singing over Sweeney's acoustic guitar, but expanded into a powerful soul ballad with a remarkable performance by the vocalist. In "One and Only," Adele sang to Poyser's gospel piano and organ — and created a modern masterpiece. (It's been reported that some of the musicians grew teary during the Malibu sessions. If so, it's likely it was during this heartbreaking performance.) "He Won't Go" built on the tension between the quick drumming and the one-per-bar piano chords; Palladino provided the rubbery funk on the bottom.

Adele recorded two tracks with Ryan Tedder, who wrote hits for Beyoncé, Taylor Swift, Carrie Underwood and many others, and is best known for his stint in OneRepublic. In "Rumor," percussion provided the primary accompaniment until strings and a blues piano arrived. "Turning Tables" was a piano ballad that profited from a gorgeous bridge buffeted by strings.

The album concluded with not with triumph, but introspection and a confession: "Somebody Like You" revealed that its narrator — and there's no reason to believe it isn't Adele speaking from the heart — hadn't recovered from her loss, though her former mate had. It was a startling exposé and the perfect conclusion to a splendid work.

In commercial terms, "21" is thus far the 21st century's most successful album. It sold more than 30 million copies worldwide, including some 10 million in the U.S., where it won Grammys for Album of the Year, Pop Vocal Album of the Year, Record and Song of the Year for "Rolling in the Deep," and Best Pop Solo Performance for "Someone Like You."

Beyond its commercial success, "21" is a brilliant achievement by an artist who embraced new influences in her quest to transform pain and a roiling emotions into a work of significant beauty and power. The result is an unforgettable recording that's worthy of all its acclaim.

Tough All Over

Gary Allan | *2005*

Allan dug
deep into his
heart
to reconnect
with life.

With "Tough All Over," Gary Allan set out to turn tragedy into art. A year before the album's release, his wife Angela committed suicide after a lengthy battle with depression. He paid tribute to her by sharing his grief with his fans.

For his sixth album, a blend of contemporary and traditional country, folk and pop, Allan covered songs that matched his somber mood. Written by Matt Scannell, the song "Best I Ever Had" revealed how Allan struggled to make sense of what was lost: "So you sailed away into a grey sky morning. And nothing's quite the same now," he sang. "Was it what you wanted?"

Throughout the album, Allan wavered between defeat and recovery. Kostas Lazarides' "Ring" permitted him to recall briefly the joy of marriage before the weight of her absence returned. But in "Promises Broken," composed by Deric Ruttan and Margaret Findley, guilt arrived without filter: "I cause tears to fall and some to lose it all/The whole world would be better off without me."

In "I Just Got Back From Hell," which he wrote with Harley Lee Allen, he addressed Satan: "Well, I've been mad at everyone including God and you/When you can't find no one to blame, you just blame yourself/And I know I'll never be the same." Then he spoke to Angela: "Forgive me if I had any part/If I ever broke your heart in two/Forgive me for what I didn't know, for what I didn't say or do." Memories linger; in "What Kind of

Fool," written by Jamie O'Hara, he sang: "I see you here, night after night, all by yourself in the blue neon light, a drink in your hand, a tear on your face."

Allan sought to reclaim his life. In "Nickajack Cave," he found inspiration in Johnny Cash's struggles and redemption. (It's said that in 1968, Cash visited the Tennessee cave intent on committing suicide. Once there, he experienced a spiritual awakening.) In the ballad "Life Ain't Always Beautiful," written by Tommy Lee James and Cyndi Goodman, he sang: "I wish for just one minute I could see your pretty face/Guess I can dream, but life don't work that way." Then he added: "Happiness has its own way of takin' its sweet time." In "Puttin' Memories Away," which Allan wrote with Matt Warren, he declared he was taking action, however reluctantly: "'Cause I'm tired of this house breakin' me down, feelin' blue/No, there's nothing left to say/I'm putting' memories away…I need to move on 'cause I know you're gone forever."

Throughout "Tough All Over," expert musicians supported Allan with sensitivity and restraint: even wall-rattlers like the title track and "No Damn Good" are delivered with reserve. Musicians chosen by producers Allan and Mark Wright for the project included Chad Cromwell, a drummer who played with Neil Young and Mark Knopfler; Robby Turner on pedal steel; and Brent Rowan on electric guitar. A B3 organ played by Steve Nathan or ex-Allman Brothers associate Reese Wynans provides a ghostly underpinning to the tracks.

Allan has released three albums of new material and two compilations since "Tough All Over" including 2013's "Set You Free," which was a critical and commercial success. In '15, his single "Hangover Tonight" suggested a new album was on its way. Thus, he resumed his career. With "Tough All Over," he dug deep into his heart and found a way to reconnect with life. That Gary Allan shared his sad adventure was, and remains, a gift to music fans.

I Am a Bird Now

Antony & the Johnsons | *2005*

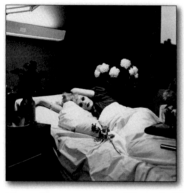

Hegarty invited intimacy as he sang in his striking, vibrato-rich voice songs of alienation and self-awareness.

In 1990, Antony Hegarty moved to New York and began performing with downtown artists, including a drag troupe known as Blacklips. Lou Reed took him under his wing and featured him on tour and his 2003 album "The Raven." Two years later, Hegarty released, as Antony & the Johnsons, "I Am A Bird Now," a remarkable chamber rock album that addressed, with beauty and disarming frankness, the issues of identity, family, and the discovery and pursuit of potential.

Though "I Am A Bird Now" was Antony & the Johnsons' second album, it served to introduce Hegarty to a wider audience following his association with Reed. A transgender youth, Hegarty said he learned "the value of emotionality and presence" during his stint with Reed. Those virtues were put to highly effective use on the first five tracks of the album: Hegarty invited intimacy as he sang in his striking, vibrato-rich voice songs of alienation and self-awareness. In the stark setting, the words landed with impact. "I'm so broken, babe," he sang in "My Lady Story, "but I want to see some shining eye." In "Hope There's Someone," he wondered from where comfort would come, both now and in eternity. In "For Today, I Am A Boy," he sang: "One day I'll grow up, I'll be a beautiful woman…/But for today I am a child, for today I am a boy…/One day, I'll grow up, I'll feel the power in me." On occasion, Hegarty shattered the quiet mood. After intermittent dissonant notes were struck in "Hope," he pounded the piano as his voice issued a vast cry.

The intimate environment changed with "You Are My Sister." Boy George joined in on vocals as bass, drums and strings assumed prominent positions. Rufus Wainwright sang and played the exquisite (and all too brief) "What Can I Do?" On "Fistful of Love," Reed spoke the lyrics until Hegarty began to sing over a backbeat that foreshadowed the soul horns and Doug Wieselman's saxophone solo. Devendra Banhart sang the opening phrases of "Spiraling."

This ad-hoc four-song suite seemed to be Hegarty's way of saying he wasn't alone; or that he and a small circle of friends shared a sense of alienation. "I was born worn, not a girl and not a jewel/I am some son, I am some bum," Hegarty sang in "Spiraling" with an understandable sense of despair. But in "You Are My Sister," he revealed, after confessing cruelty to a loved one, how profound intimacy can be: "You lived inside my world so softly/Protected only by the kindness of your nature" and "There's nothing left to gain from remembering faces and world that no one else will ever know."

With a glimmer of hope, "Bird Gerhl" brought the album to a lovely conclusion as Hegarty sang over a piano, folk guitar and strings: "I've got my heart in my hands now/I've been searching for my wings.../'Cause I'm a bird girl and bird girls go to heaven."

"I Am A Bird" won the Mercury Prize for best album — Hegarty was eligible because he was born in Chichester, U.K. His career was already in bloom. A frequent and ambitious collaborator, he worked with Björk, Marianne Faithfull and Oneohtrix Point Never; appeared in the film "Leonard Cohen: I'm Your Man"; and his version of Bob Dylan's "Knockin' on Heaven's Door" was a highlight of the soundtrack album to Todd Haynes' film "I'm Not There." He sang his composition "Angel on Fire" on the soundtrack to "The Hunger Games: Catching Fire." His albums that followed "I Am A Bird" — particularly "Swanlights," issued in 2010 — reinforced his standard of excellence.

With "I Am A Bird," Hegarty conveyed the emotional complexity of his journey toward self-discovery and realization, and did so with transcendent beauty and passion.

Extraordinary Machine

Fiona Apple | *2005*

It was old meets new in the best sense: without sentiment and moving toward an innovative form of expression.

When an album's release is delayed repeatedly, it's usually not a sign that what's held in abeyance is an exceptional piece of music. Not so with Fiona Apple's "Extraordinary Machine," which, upon release, was recognized immediately as a quirky and beautiful gem.

The saga: a version of the album was completed in May 2003; after additional recording by Apple and producer Jon Brion, the release date was postponed until early 2004. Tracks began to leak via the web, and a bootleg copy emerged in late February 2005, followed by more tracks without an official issue date. Finally, with new production by Mike Elizondo and Brian Kehew, "Extraordinary Machine" was released September 30, 2005. Turned out the delay was a case of making what was very good even better.

The marriage of Apple's songs and the bewitching arrangements was perfection — it was old meets new in the best sense: without sentiment and moving toward an innovative form of expression. With her voice and piano as the centerpiece, Apple and her team borrowed from chamber pop, Weimar-era cabaret music and industrial rock to shape the sound. "Tymps (The Sick in the Head Song)" features what might've been tiny hammers, handclaps and a zither. The underpinning of "Window" opened with what sounded like bubbling liquid in a heated beaker; at the bridge, a bass joined in and reeds tooted in the background. Whirling strings, clarinets and trumpets colored "Waltz (Better Than Fine)." While "Not About Love" swayed on a piano pattern and light tapping on the cymbals until the music took jolting turns. "Parting Gift" was a stark boozy ballad, as was "Red Red Red"; the latter featured a chilly orchestra. The intriguing arrangements suited the melodies, which Apple delivered with confidence and a touch of insouciance that suited her lyrics.

Some of Apple's words appeared to be commentary on the hesitant recording process. In the title track, she sang: "I'm good at being uncomfortable so I can't stop changing all the time" and "I seem to you to seek a new disaster every day...I mean to prove I mean to move in my own way." And in the finale "Waltzing (Better Than Fine)": "No I don't believe in wasting time, but I don't believe I'm wasting mine" and "Everyone else's goal's to get big-headed/Why should I follow that beat being that I'm better than fine?"

In between, there were songs about the trauma of love, often told with an unexpected twist and delightfully dated phrase. "One man he disappoint me/He give me the gouge and he take my glee.../Wait 'til I get him back/He won't have a back to scratch." Throughout the album, Apple emerged as a keen-eyed character who, though stung, moved on, better and wiser for the experience.

Apple toured behind "Extraordinary Machine," opening for Coldplay for a while before headlining on a tour that lasted from spring to autumn of 2006. Well-received by critics and snatched up by eager fans, the album sold well, achieving gold status. Since then, Apple has released only one other album; known as "The Idler Wheel," it actually has 23 words in its title. It came out in 2012, seven years after the "Extraordinary Machine," proving that Apple likes to take her time. With "Extraordinary Machine," the wait was worth it. It's a fascinating achievement.

Funeral

Arcade Fire | *2004*

One of
the most
exceptional
albums of
the 21st
century —
for its inherent
qualities and
its inadvertent
timeliness

In 2001, Arcade Fire was formed in Montreal by Win Butler and Josh Deu, who met at Philips Exeter Academy. Régine Chassagne joined early on, and they went to work. The result: "Funeral," the band's debut, released in 2004. It remains one of the most exceptional albums of the 21st century — for its inherent qualities and its inadvertent timeliness.

Unprecedented and thus unexpected, "Funeral" was a blend of various rock and folk forms, delivered in lurching and scurrying tempos, in the service of high drama: the return to a new normalcy after the death of loved ones. Built largely on chugging guitars and clattering percussion, the music derived its abundant colors from sheets of sound featuring accordion, xylophone, violin, French horn, recorder, bass, piano and a battery of synths, thus bringing together Acadian folk, indie rock and soul. The story was told from a childlike perspective — perhaps the narrators are in their late teens or even younger than that — and the emotional, strained, occasionally reckless lead vocals, mostly by Butler, gave a sense of urgency to the struggle to manage grief. Chassagne added a sweet touch of harmony now and again, and backing vocals swelled to contribute to the vast, stirring backdrop.

The album also had unintended implications. It arrived in the aftermath of the September 11 attacks in the U.S. and 10 months before the July 7 bombings in London. To be clear, "Funeral" had nothing to do with the terrorist attacks: it was about the band members' private sorrows, specifically the death of three family members shortly before and while the songs were composed. But its themes of death, the ensuing emptiness, the slow realization that recovery is possible, and the search for a way back to joy mirrored universal experiences. Thus, it was an invaluable work of art.

Metaphors abounded. The album opened with "And if the snow buries my neighborhood/And if my parents are crying/Then I'll dig a tunnel from my window to yours." In the second track, an older brother Alexander, lost to illness or despair, was encouraged to pull through: "For a year we caught his tears in a cup/And now we're going to make him drink it/Come on, Alex, don't die or dry up." In "Neighborhood #3 (Power Out)," Butler sang of addressing his own grief, as a melancholy violin soared over rumbling percussion and sheets of synthesized sound, the music reinforced the tension between the narrator and the world around him.

Slowly, the mood changed. "Neighborhood #4," a persistent folk tune enriched by strings, concluded with: "Just like a seed down in the soil, you've got to give time." Next came "Crown of Love," sung against the chiming of an old piano: "They say it fades if you let it...I carved your name across my eyelids." Later in the song, as the band bursts into double time, Mr. Butler sang: "Your name is the only word I can say."

"Wake Up" provided a sense of catharsis. Everything wasn't all right — "Something filled my heart up with nothing," Butler sang — but there was the recognition of the future, however uncertain, as a piano and a Motown backbeat kicked in and the celebratory music delivered a feeling of relief. In the next tune, Chassagne sang: "All the tears and all the bodies bring about our second birth."

"Funeral" closed with "Rebellion (Lies)," Arcade Fire's tightest performance to that point; and "In the Backseat," a touching piece of chamber pop with lovely strings. In the former, Butler sang: "Now here's the sun/It's all right/Now here's the moon/It's all right." In the latter, after declaring she enjoyed the perspective from the backseat where she could watch the world pass by without responsibility, Ms. Chassagne sang: "My family tree is losing all its leaves." As the song began to fade, she added: "I've been learning to drive/My whole life I've been learning."

In the aftermath of "Funeral," which won the Grammy for Album of the Year, Arcade Fire became, and continues to be, one of rock's most popular and consistently intriguing acts. If their 2007 "Neon Bible" was a letdown, it was only because of the brilliance of its predecessor, which won the Grammy for Album of the Year. Their 2010 album "The Suburbs" is an underrated gem, and their '13 disc "Reflektor," the band's take on contemporary dance music, adds to their legacy. But "Funeral" is their masterwork, for what it is and how it can be applied.

Whatever People Say I Am, That's What I'm Not

Arctic Monkeys | 2006

High-energy, wall-rattling rock accompanied Alex Turner's sharp-tongued tales.

Arctic Monkeys' debut album "Whatever People Say I Am, That's What I'm Not" established immediately the Sheffield, U.K-based group as a formidable unit. The rock quartet's powerful sound, and Alex Turner's savvy lyrics, concealed their youth: lead singer and guitarist Turner had just turned 20 years old when the album was released, and guitarist Jamie Cook and bassist Andy Nicholson weren't much older. Drummer Matt Helders was 19. The group had been together for four years, and they were tight and authoritative to the point of cockiness. As a lyricist, Turner had an intriguing point of view that grounded the music in the workaday world. The album would have been an achievement for a veteran group well into their career.

"Whatever People Say I Am, That's What I'm Not" balanced punk and the kind of driving, melodic Britpop played so well by Blur, Oasis and fellow Sheffield natives Pulp. Driven by Helders, who emerged as a great rock drummer from the album's opening moments, the band built their instrumental sound around a two-guitar attack, Nicholson's range on the bottom and the pleasure of tricky arrangements. With "I Bet You Look Good on the Dancefloor," a number-one hit single in the U.K., the band led with tempered rage. But by "Fake Tales of San Francisco," the album's third track, Arctic Monkeys demonstrated that their sound that would allow the group to roam from repetition. In "Still Take You Home" and "You

Probably Couldn't See For The Lights But You Were Staring Straight At Me," the band tossed in bits of a heavy surf rock in a punk setting.

The album's title was a line culled from Allan Sillitoe's 1958 novel "Saturday Night and Sunday Morning," later a film starring Albert Finney. Though many of the songs had already been written for the album before he came upon the story, Turner saw that Sillitoe's novel drew its spark from what he was writing about: how working-class people need to blow off steam, which on occasion results in regrettable behavior and dire consequences. Turner focused on his night-life theme to the point where some reviewers considered "Whatever People Say I Am, That's What I'm Not" a concept album. As it was with Sillitoe and other so-called "angry young men" novelists and playwrights in the 1950s England, Turner, whose insouciance as a vocalist was perfect for his lyrics, viewed his subjects with a jarring blend of affection and scorn.

High-energy, wall-rattling rock accompanied Turner's sharp-tongued tales, though "When the Sun Goes Down" opened and ended as an oily ballad in which the narrator observed a meeting of a streetwalker and "scummy man." He sang: "Although you're trying not to listen/Avert your eyes and staring at the ground/She makes a subtle proposition/...He must be up to something." In "Fake Tales of San Francisco," Turner ripped a band from a few towns over for putting on airs by boasting of an American tour it hadn't taken. As for a female fan who adores the bogus band, he sang: "Love's not only blind but deaf."

"Whatever People Say I Am, That's What I'm Not" launched Arctic Monkeys to a high-flying career that continues today. The first of their five studio full-length albums, it won the 2006 Mercury Prize as the best album from the U.K. and Ireland. It sold well from the moment it was available and is said to be the fastest-selling debut disc by a U.K. band. One of the best first albums in rock history, "Whatever People Say I Am, That's What I'm Not" remains a smart, powerful collection that served to foreshadow the subsequent music by the band built for the long run.

Mama's Gun

Erykah Badu | *2000*

Badu once again blended schools of funk, R&B, jazz and rock with deceptive ease.

For her second album, singer-composer Erykah Badu was faced with the challenge of creating a work comparable to her massive hit debut "Baduizm," issued in 1997. Regarded as a benchmark of neo-soul, "Baduizm" sold more than three million copies in the U.S. and won a well-deserved Grammy as Best R&B Album. After giving birth to a son, Badu stepped away from music until 1999 when she returned to recording in the studio. The result was "Mama's Gun." The 2000 album is the artistic equal of its predecessor and confirmed Badu's status as a major figure in contemporary music.

On "Mama's Gun," Badu once again blended schools of funk, R&B, jazz and rock with deceptive ease, often within the same song. Her vocals were superb; on "Baduizm," she was compared to Billie Holiday, which wasn't all that apt — except for their mutual talent for swinging behind the beat and finding the most sensual delivery for the lyric. Badu was at ease in every musical setting. Produced by J Dilla, "Didn't Cha Know" added a dab of Latin percussion to a quicksilvery soul ballad that flowed seamlessly into the snap-funk of "My Life," which rode on a repeated piano riff and lovely strings. Tight funk horns added color to "Booty" while "A.D. 2000" rose from a strummed acoustic guitar. "Penitentiary Philosophy" was a raging rock with an undercurrent of slinky funk.

Jazz helped shape "Mama's Bag." "… & On" featured a jazz interlude and layered scatting, and vibraphonist Roy Ayers was the guest on "Cleva," which had a Stevie Wonder feel. On several tracks, Roy Hargrove played trumpet and arranged the horns. Jack DeJohnette's "Epilogue" was sampled for "Kiss on My Neck" and excerpts from Johnny "Hammond" Smith's "Gambler's Life" appeared in "Booty" and "Bag Lady."

Badu was a member of an ad-hoc group of musicians known as the Soulquarians, and her colleagues James Poyser and Ahmir "Questlove" Thompson created the supple spine of her sound. Pino Palladino played bass; as always, he was splendid. On the folk ballad "In Love With You," Badu shared the spotlight with Stephen Marley, her duet partner.

Throughout "Mama's Gun," Badu chose to present herself in the starkest terms to her audience, and the closer it looked, the more complex an artist it found in plain view: wise, sly, defiant, mischievous; a young woman fully formed yet evolving. "You can't win when your will is weak," she sang in "Penitentiary Philosophy" — a line that seemed to be her motto. Resolve mattered more than appearance, in "Cleva," she sang: "My dress ain't cost nothin' but seven dollars, but I made it fly and I'll tell you why. I'm cleva when I bust a rhyme." She revealed her occasional uncertainty: "I'm insecure… My mind says more, my heart lags behind/But I don't love you any more" is how she phrased it in "My Eyes Are Green." The gorgeous ballad "Orange Moon" may be an homage to her firstborn. Or it may reflect her interest in the spiritual philosophies of the Five Percent Nation: "I'm an orange moon/ I'm brighter than before, brighter/Reflecting the light of the sun."

In the years following "Mama's Gun," Badu's music remains vital and as a result, she's put together a body of work that's as impressive as any of her contemporaries. Eminently musical, intriguing and deliciously sophisticated, "Mama's Gun" presented an artist at ease with her music and her complicated self.

Beyoncé

Beyoncé | *2013*

The arrival of "Beyoncé" caught the industry and her fans off guard.

On December 13, 2013, the new album by Beyoncé turned up unannounced on iTunes in a package that included 14 tracks and 17 videos. It was an instant hit, becoming the fastest-selling album in the history of Apple's music service. In the U.S., it was Beyoncé's fifth consecutive number-one album.

The innovative rollout and the immediate success stole away a bit of the limelight from the music: "Beyoncé" is a remarkable album by the era's greatest R&B and pop artist. It's a bold statement on the status and plight of women in contemporary culture.

Beyoncé Knowles had worked her way to excellence, finding international acclaim with the group Destiny's Child, which she joined before her teen years. Prior to their break-up in 2006, the trio's albums sold some 60 million copies. She worked on independent projects and released her first solo album in 2003: "Dangerously in Love" confirmed that a new mega-star was at hand, as did her appearances in the film version of "Dreamgirls," playing the role based on Diana Ross; and in "Cadillac Records," in which Knowles portrayed Etta James. No singer had more Top 10 hits in the 2000s.

Because Knowles was amid what would become a 132-date tour, the arrival of "Beyoncé" caught the industry and her fans off guard. So did the album's dark lyrical themes. In her previous album, "4," issued in 2011, she espoused personal responsibility and commitment to family, suggesting they would lead to deep contentment, and its crisp contemporary R&B boosted the bright, breezy theme. But on "Beyoncé," she wrote and sang, often in raw, explicit terms, about self-doubt, rejection, self-image, gnawing dissatisfaction and overt sexuality — the latter most notably in the Jacksonesque "Blow" and in the simmering "Drunk in Love," which featured an appearance by Jay Z, her husband.

The album opened with the booming voice of Harvey Keitel asking: "What is your aspiration in life?" In a halting voice, Knowles replied, "My aspiration in life would be to be happy" — as if she knows it's a goal that's out of reach. As the song unfolded, we learned she's been told, "What's in your head doesn't matter… What you wear is all that matters." Her voice soaring, at the bridge she declared that the pursuit of image, and believing it is so, leaves one empty and unfulfilled: "Plastic smiles and denials can only take you so far/Then you break when the fake façade leaves you in the dark."

The seemingly experimental nature of the album's musical platform was advanced in "Ghost/Haunting" in which she spoke, with a voice that dripped with disgust and discontent, of the tedium of a career in the recording industry. But then the song opened into a ballad over sparse, Aphex Twin-inspired beats by Boots that married hip hop and dubstep. In "No Angel," a song about sex and marital discord, she sang over swooshing synths, an insinuating bass line and colliding beats; a passing lyric connected the song to the theme introduced in "Pretty Hurts," the album opener: "Know I'm not the girl you thought you knew and that you wanted/ Underneath the pretty face is something complicated."

Knowles used well the guests she invited to participate in "Beyoncé." Drake provided the counterpoint on the piano ballad "Mine," rapping over clacking percussion. "Superpower" was a modern take on doo-wop, with Knowles singing over chiming voices and kettle drums; Frank Ocean joined in with a rap-sung interlude. In "Flawless," she employed a speech by the Nigerian poet Chimamanda Ngozi Adichie, who entered with a perspective that challenged gender-based bias.

Knowles concluded the album with two affecting piano ballads, both of which return to the theme of the importance of family: though it hasn't been confirmed, it's believed that "Heaven" is about the child Knowles lost to a miscarriage. "Blue" is dedicated to her daughter: "When I'm holding you tight, I'm so alive." She delivered beautifully, as the emotion of the song flowed gently toward the listener.

A brave and exceptional effort, "Beyoncé" had much to say about women and how their identities are formed — ideas that are delivered in a manner that provokes the listener to ponder them well after the music is put away.

Vespertine

Björk | *2005*

Björk declared that there was no border between pop and the avant garde.

From the opening moments of the song "Hidden Place," in which she placed a traditional melody over scratchy, pulsing electronics, choral voices, orchestral strings, flutes and a sample from Schoenberg, Björk declared with "Vespertine" that there was no border between pop and the avant garde, and thus there were no rules that must be obeyed.

For Björk Guðmundsdóttir, "Vespertine" represented yet another advance in her approach to popular song. She began her recording career before she became a teenager, and in 1987 joined the Sugarcubes, a supergroup in Iceland, her homeland. The band released three albums in the U.S. and U.K., thus introducing Björk to a wider audience. In 1993, she issued "Debut," considered her first solo album.

"Debut" revealed what would become Björk's modus operandi: she placed herself at the center of a collaborative effort build on her compositions and a specific idea of what she wanted in her arrangements. The guests on "Debut" included jazz saxophonist Oliver Lake and a battery of programmers featuring Nellee Hooper; formally trained, Björk played keyboards and programmed synthesized bass and brass lines. Her voice — full of intelligence and youthful charm — more than held its own in a complex environment. Buoyed by five singles, including the wonderful "Venus as a Boy," the album sold more than one million copies in the U.S.

"Post" and "Homogenic" followed, as did two remix albums and "Selmasongs," the soundtrack to "Dancer in the Dark," the Lars von Trier film in which she starred. She began work on "Vespertine" in 2000.

The album was born out of several ideas or reactions. Having grown tired of bass-heavy electronic percussion, Björk wanted some high-end sounds as a platform: celesta, harp and chiming music boxes were featured. She crafted new sounds to create new beats, using the crackle of ice breaking or the snap of shuffled cards. She found inspiration in the music of Thomas Knak, who works as Opiate, and Martin Gretschmann. And she had fallen in love, thus leading to romantic, often intimate lyrics: sex and domesticity were repeated themes. In full control of the project, Björk arranged the beats, choir, strings and universe of new sounds, placing her voice in an intimate environment best described as enchanting. In "Harm of Will," she sang accompanied by bells, music boxes, an orchestra and choir. In "Unison," she appeared to be singing to an orchestra of toys.

The music was at original and yet once vaguely familiar, as if it had always existed in some magical elsewhere and was now here. In "Cocoon," a synthesized bass and what sounded like static electricity provided the initial underpinning: the artificial and the organic merged to inform the new. Similarly, "It's Not Up To You" opened with a mix of natural and synthetic sounds; a wave of strings and harp glissandos arrived to sweep under Björk's voice, which was joined by a choir.

In "Pagan Poetry," the chiming was more assertive, as many voices — all Björk's, overdubbed — rose in counterpoint, and a bass pulsed; and then the music stopped as she repeated "I love him" without accompaniment until voices whispered "She loves him" and strings returned. "Heirloom" seemed to reach back for what she dubbed "thumping techno," only in a lighter, more temperate version featuring a pumping bass. She sang patiently over a variety of sound effects and treated voices in "Sun in My Mouth" and "An Echo, a Stain."

"Vespertine" sold well, though not by the standards of "Debut." (Napster and file sharing had seeped in by the time it was released.) It was number one on the charts in Denmark, France and Spain, and in the top three in several other countries. She went on a lengthy tour, which was captured on "Vespertine Live," issued in 2004, and has since released four more studio albums.

With her body of work, of which "Vespertine" is a highlight, Björk confirms she is a singular artist and one of the greatest rock and pop musicians of her era, and beyond.

Spirit of the Century

The Blind Boys of Alabama | *2001*

Secular music was infused with gospel's soul.

The Blind Boys of Alabama first sang together in the early 1940s, the same decade in which some of the songwriters and musicians on their "Spirit of the Century" were born: John Hammond, Mick Jagger, Keith Richards, David Lindley, Charlie Musselwhite and Tom Waits. On the album, Blind Boys original members Clarence Fountain, Jimmy Carter and George Scott took the secular music and, with their gruff, honey-thick vocal harmonies, infused it with gospel's soul.

"Spirit of the Century" was the brainchild of producer John Chelew, who also brought to the project bassist Danny Thompson and drummer Michael Jerome. Chelew said Fountain wanted the Blind Boys to study the lyrics before proceeding. They found the link between traditional gospel themes and the messages in the modern material.

Waits' "Jesus Gonna Be Here" opened the disc and sets the template by placing Fountain's voice in a loose, bluesy environment with Thompson's upright bass providing the limber spine for the track. The Blind Boys' performance of Ben Harper's "Give a Man a Home" straddled the sacred and the secular by blending fiery gospel and contemporary rock-blues; it featured a harmonica solo by Musselwhite. The Rolling Stones' "Just Wanna See His Face" rose from Jerome's drumming, a tambourine on the downbeat and, again, Musselwhite's harmonica. The most familiar track on the album, and one that represented it well, was the Blind Boys' take on Waits' "Down in the Hole."

A slinky blues featuring Carter on lead vocal, it served as theme for HBO's "The Wire" during its opening season.

New interpretations of gospel standards were at the album's core. Scott's baritone rumbled on an exceptional reading of "Run on for a Long Time," and the group's voices rose in harmony above Hammond's Dobro on "Nobody's Fault But Mine." "Good Religion" was treated as country blues. And in what may have been the album's most remarkable track, the group sang "Amazing Grace" over the chords to "House of the Rising Sun," suggesting that redemption is always at hand, even in a den of ill repute.

"Spirit of the Century," which was released on Peter Gabriel's Real World label, served to introduce the Blind Boys of Alabama to a new audience and revitalized their lengthy career. Road warriors for seven decades, they toured behind the album, only this time they were playing venues typically reserved for rock acts. (They retained their long-time habit of entering the halls from the rear and walking down the aisle in single file, a hand on the shoulder of the man before them.) Scott died in 2005 and Fountain retired from live performance due to health issues, but Carter remains with the Blind Boys, who have added members as needed to the front line — including Bobby Butler, Ricky McKinnie and Joey Williams — and the backing band. In subsequent recordings, they continued to explore the commonalities among some contemporary songs and traditional gospel.

In 2002, "Spirit of the Century" won the Grammy for Best Traditional Soul Gospel Album, and a year later the Blind Boys of Alabama were inducted into the Gospel Music Hall of Fame, an honor that was long overdue.

Beyond the lift it gave the Blind Boys of Alabama, "Spirit of the Century" introduced fans of Gabriel, Harper, Waits, the Rolling Stones and the other contributors to gospel standards performed by one of the genre's greatest groups. Thus, the album fulfilled the mission of a crossover recording by satisfying two constituencies, both of whom profited from the splendid effort.

Dig, Lazarus, Dig!!!

Nick Cave & The Bad Seeds | *2008*

The freewheeling music matched perfectly Cave's sordid tales.

"Dig, Lazarus, Dig!!!" was a torrent of stories set to music. The Bad Seeds provided the nasty, kaleidoscopic sounds while Nick Cave wrote the tales that rose from a gothic, nightmarish view of contemporary life among denizens of the night. Wit and terror resided side by side, as did innocence and deceit.

"Lazarus" was the 14th studio album by Cave and the band, and by then he had a well-developed and much-admired reputation as a concert performer with an on-stage personality somewhere between suave and louche with an ample dose of tent preacher tossed in. Cave began his career in Melbourne in his native Australia with covers of David Bowie, Lou Reed, Roxy Music and others who continued as influences through much of his career. The Bad Seeds formed in 1983, and multi-instrumentalist Warren Ellis joined in '94. Cave and Ellis have recorded 10 soundtracks for film and theater, perhaps most notably for "The Road," the film based on the Cormac McCarthy novel of the same name.

One constant on the many albums by the Bad Seeds was Cave's writing. He had a way with imagery and character that created a sense of intimacy even while suggesting danger and rabid discontent. Perhaps it's no surprise that, in addition to his work in film as a composer, he also wrote screenplays, including one for John Hillcoat's "The Proposition" — he also wrote a sequel to "Gladiator" that his friend Russell Crowe hated — and published two novels.

In "Dig, Lazarus, Dig!!!" Cave's many skills as a writer coalesced in lyrics that were rhythmic, cinematic and literate. The freewheeling, careening music matched perfectly his sordid tales, all of which seemed to unfold in a drug-fueled world on the other side of a gauzy veil.

The album opened with a tale of modern Lazarus, known as Larry. "But Larry grew increasing neurotic and obscene/I mean, he never asked to be raised from the tomb," Cave sang as guitars rasped below. In "Midnight Man," a tale rife with unsettling images, he sang: "Wolves have carried your babies away/...You spread yourself like a penitent upon the mad vibrating sand." Darting keyboards reinforced the a disorienting environment.

Cave often questioned in song his own faith in a higher power, and in the third-person "We Call Upon the Author," he declared: "Everything is messed up around here/Everything is banal and jejune/...Well, he knew exactly who to blame." But Cave may be a character who is upset with an author's design for him. Or he may be writer unhappy with the state of literature: name-checking Bukowski, Berryman and Hemingway, he sang: "I see they've published another volume of unreconstructed rubbish." Staticky guitar squealed, and he offered a solution that covered all possibilities: "Prolix! Prolix! There's nothing a pair of scissors can't fix." In the drowsy "More News from Nowhere," Cave spun a tale of a man who women entice, terrify and reject. "Don't it make you feel alone," he sang. "Don't it make you want to get right back home." The album's last line is "Well, I got to say, goodbye."

In the immediate aftermath of "Lazarus," Cave and members of the Bad Seeds released a second album as Grinderman, which took its name from a Memphis Slim song. In 2013, Cave & the Bad Seeds issued "Push the Sky Away," a contemplative album dripping with menace in which Cave sang over moody, carefully wrought electronic-based tracks. The year 2014 saw the arrival of "20,000 Days on Earth," a film about Cave that presented a fictional account of a day in his life while recording "Push the Sky Away." Ellis provided the music.

Though much came before and continued since, with "Dig, Lazarus, Dig!!!" Nick Cave & the Bad Seeds made the best album of his, and their adventurous career.

Voodoo

D'Angelo | *2000*

An innovative masterwork from a superior, independent musician.

In the last decades of the 20th century, the term "neo soul" came into vogue to describe a style of music made primarily by African-Americans that drew from the rich veins of funk, gospel, hip hop, jazz, R&B and traditional soul. In concert and on their free-flowing recordings, Erykah Badu, Bilal, Macy Gray, Lauryn Hill, Maxwell, Meshell Ndegeocello and others who were referred to as neo-soul artists acknowledged the influence of Roberta Flack, Marvin Gaye, Donny Hathaway, Curtis Mayfield, Prince, Gil Scott-Heron, Nina Simone, Stevie Wonder and others by taking forward what their gifted predecessors had created.

The greatest album of the so-called "neo soul" period is D'Angelo's "Voodoo." Unexpected — at times startlingly so — it presented an abundantly talented artist who knew well the history but had decided to go off to find a new mode of expression. The result was a work that satisfied body, mind and spirit.

"Voodoo" was the second album by Michael Eugene Archer under his stage name; in 1995, he issued "Brown Sugar," which sold more than a million copies and was nominated for four Grammys. D'Angelo played almost all the instruments on his debut, blending silky jazz and funk with hip-hop rhythms. An orchestra accompanied him on Smokey Robinson's "Cruisin'" and jazz musicians Larry Grenadier, Gene Lake and Mark Whitefield sat in on the slinky, undeniable "Smooth." But fully equipped and fully in control, the album was D'Angelo's showcase.

In a move that presaged how he would managed his career,

D'Angelo then disappeared for more than four years, resurfacing to contribute to film soundtracks. "Voodoo" arrived in January 2000. It was at the same time sparse and rich, harmonically complex and groove-driven, and doodle-loose to the edge of disintegration. The opening track "Playa Playa" served as template: a riveting bass figure by Pino Palladino held the track together while Roy Hargrove's muted trumpet floated in the distance. Palladino and Hargrove, along with drummer Ahmir "Questlove" Thompson tapped into more traditional soul on "Send It On." D'Angelo played all the instruments on the bluesy "Devil's Pie," in which he layered his voice and sang deliciously behind the beat. Rappers Method Man and Redman joined in on the hypnotic "Left & Right," which featured D'Angelo on funk guitar and rubbery bass.

At its midpoint, "Voodoo" veered in a different direction with tracks that were more full-bodied. Charlie Hunter played the bass and solo guitar parts on the down-tempo "The Root" and in the medley of "Greatdayindamornin'" and "Booty," which profited from Thompson's clever patterns on the kick drum and cymbals. Written by D'Angelo and Hargrove, "Spanish Joint" walked the line between soul and jazz-funk, and his cover of Gene McDaniels' "Feel Like Makin' Love," a huge hit for Flack, rode on a Palladino-Thompson groove that permitted D'Angelo to sing and scat as Hargrove's horn snaked around him.

"Voodoo" concluded with "Untitled (How Does It Feel)," a performance that was taut with sexual tension, and "Africa," a celebration of heritage and home. In both numbers, D'Angelo's brilliance as a soul singer was confirmed, though by that time it didn't need to be.

"Voodoo" was a commercial success too, outselling "Brown Sugar" and winning a Grammy for Best R&B album. D'Angelo toured widely with Alford, Hargrove, Palladino and Thompson; keyboard player James Poyser (of the Roots) and trumpeter Russell Gunn were among those who joined the ensemble known as the Soultronics.

At the tour's end, D'Angelo withdrew again. In late 2014, he issued, without advance warning, "Black Messiah," a splendid album that revealed he still had the power to create lean, textured funk that was intellectually and emotionally complex.

Prior to the release of "Black Messiah," D'Angelo was interviewed by Nelson George at the Brooklyn Museum. The conversation turned to the term "neo soul." D'Angelo said, "I think the main thing about the whole neo-soul thing, not to put it down...but you want to be in a position where you can grow as an artist...I never claimed I do neo soul, you know. I used to always say, 'I do black music. I make black music.'"

The Grey Album

Danger Mouse | *2004*

The Beatles' classical album underwent a hip-hop tune-up.

Mashups — songs that are created out of two or more existing songs — have been around since the mid-1950s. "The Grey Album" by Danger Mouse, released in 2004, is the best-known album of such combo tracks. Its source material: "The Black Album" by Jay Z and "The Beatles," also known as the White Album. The marriage of black and white to create grey seems obvious, a gimmick at best. But "The Grey Album" works both musically and as challenge to fans who think rap and classic rock can't co-exist.

At the point when "The Grey Album" was released, Danger Mouse was all but unknown to the mainstream, either under his stage handle or as Brian Burton, his name at birth. He released trip-hop tracks as Pelican City, remixed various cuts and worked as a DJ before creating the Danger Mouse persona. In 2003, he released an album with Jemini the Gifted One.

On "The Grey Album," he revealed his thorough knowledge of popular music history and his own musicality. (Burton plays a variety of instruments, most notably the drums, which accounts for his keen sense of time.) The payoff was immediate: on the album's opening track, he married Jay Z's "Public Service Announcement" with George Harrison's "Long, Long, Long." Jay Z dominated the top line and underneath his rap a piano on "The Black Album" original fit tight a riff Harrison played on acoustic guitar. Thus, 2003 and 1968, the years the Jay Z and Beatles albums were released, respectively, came together flawlessly. A point had been made to snobs on either side of the rock vs. rap argument.

Paul McCartney's piano introduction to Harrison's "While My Guitar Gently Weeps" ushered in "What More Can I Say" and Eric Clapton's guitar on the former rang through. The strings in the Jay Z original are reminiscent of the sweep into the bridge of the Harrison song. Danger Mouse re-edited "Happiness Is a Warm Gun" for "Moment of Clarity" and isolated McCartney's acoustic guitar in the gentle "Mother Nature's Son" for the fit with "December 4th." Fans of John Lennon's "Julia" might've been shocked by Jay Z's profane entrance over the song's fingerpicked acoustic guitar, but the track settled down and worked too.

The collision of "Helter Skelter" and "99 Problems" was pushed by Danger Mouse's rejiggering of Ringo Starr's unmistakable drums. When Jay Z yelled "Hit Me," the space was filled by wall of guitar riffs. (The use of Starr's shout "I got blisters on my fingers" on the original might've been too cheesy.) The mashup of the Beatles' "Glass Onion" and "Savoy Truffle" with Jay Z's "Encore" featured a rap cooking in double time that was surrounded by a bed of electric guitars and Lennon's repeated moan "Oh yeah."

Danger Mouse issued "The Grey Album" via a few websites, but it soon caught on. Jay Z had released an a cappella version of "The Black Album" to aid producers in using it in remixes; he called "The Grey Album" "a genius idea." The Beatles' label, EMI, did not approve, but McCartney and Starr didn't protest, at least not vehemently. "The record company minded," McCartney said. "They put up a fuss. But it was like, 'Take it easy, guys, it's a tribute.'"

Danger Mouse's career has blossomed. He formed Gnarls Barkley with Cee-Lo Green, Broken Bells with James Mercer, and produced albums by Beck, the Black Keys, Gorillaz, Norah Jones, Portugal. The Man and others, winning five Grammys along the way. But it was the mashup disc, "The Grey Album," that introduced him to the rock world. It's a bright idea, beautifully executed.

Deli

Victor Démé | *2010*

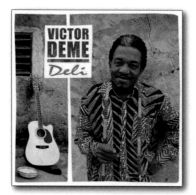

From West Africa an album with a world full of delights

Burkina Faso's Victor Démé released his first album in 2008 after decades of performing in clubs and festivals in West Africa, particularly Côte d'Ivoire and, when the political climate allowed, at home. When his self-titled debut was issued, Démé was 46. Two years later, he followed with "Deli," a thrilling collection that comprise not only West African ballads, but folk, gospel, Latin rock and the blues.

The album set out to seduce listeners. It opened with "Hine Ye Deli Le La," a swaying ballad that worked the territory made familiar in the West by Salif Keita of Mali: acoustic guitars, Dimitri Artemenko's violin and Salif Diarra's kora were among the instruments that embraced Démé's voice. "Teban Siyala" deployed a similar musical environment, albeit with the addition of a drum kit explored gently. Fixi's accordion and hand drums supported the melodrama of "Méka Déen," while "Deen Wolo Mousso" unfolded like American folk-rock with more than a touch of the blues. The latter's sing-along chorus made the listener wish he understood the Mandinka language.

Démé's sense of self-possession carried the album. Regardless of the tweaks to the setting, he remained the centerpiece. Propelled by shakers and hand drums, "Banaiba" raced ahead and so did "Séré Jugu," this time with an electric guitar as the pulse: even when the music grew aggressive, Démé conveyed a calm that held off a storm.

Much of the final third of "Deli" sounds as if it was recorded at a different studio with many Western-minded pop musicians. "Wolo Baya Guéléma," which features Femi Kuti on saxophone, is a fair approximation of an early Santana jam set in West Africa. Guitars and electric bass added a blithe background to "Sina," a showcase for violinist Artemenko and clarinetist Lionel Messas. "Maa Gaafora" was an American-style country blues with Damien Tartamella on harmonica while "Ma Belle" is a funky love song in which an acoustic guitar and trombone flit over hand drums. But Démé returned to some of the traditional sounds of West Africa for the album closer, "Tan Ni Kéléen," which employ a kora and an army of percussion for its hypnotic underpinning; female voices engaged in call-and-response with the singer.

If Démé has released a follow-up album to "Deli," it's yet to reach the U.S. He played his first U.S. show in New York's Central Park in 2012 — where he won over a crowd of devotees of Jimmy Cliff, the headliner — but he hasn't done a full tour in the States. In 2014, the French techno duo known as Synapson issued an engaging four-track collection of house-style remixes Démé's "Djon Maya Mai," a track on his debut disc. For all the allure of the dance mixes by Synapson, Sascha Braemer, Oliver Koletzki and Niko Scwhind, the tracks serve to remind us of the joy and wonder in Démé's voice, and compels us to listen to "Deli," an album rich with delights from an artist the wide world has yet to discover.

An End Has A Start

Editors | *2007*

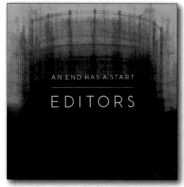

Gloom,
anxiety,
pessimism,
but never
helplessness

Editors arrived in 2005 out of Birmingham, England, with a series of successful singles and, a year later, their debut album, "The Back Room." The group was compared to Echo & The Bunnymen, Joy Division, the Smiths, early U2 and other smart, dark alt-rock and post-punk groups. This is high praise for newcomers, and with their second album "An End Has A Start," Editors created a work that fulfilled their promise.

There were no moments of hesitation or uncertainty on "An End Has a Start," yet nothing felt as if it was overcooked. Vocalist Tom Smith sang with steely control, his baritone serving in juxtaposition to the band's shimmering performances, particularly in the stirring ballads "Push Your Head Towards the Air," "The Weight of the World" and "Well Worn Hand." When raw emotion was needed, Smith delivered too: he sounded like he was about to lift off the earth in "Escape the Nest," singing as the music and his words required.

Whether the subject was something within or what he's observed, Smith's lyrics revealed that his perspective was coated in gloom, anxiety and pessimism. But never hopelessness: love may not be the answer, but it existed. Demonstrating a gift for metaphor, his writing on "An End Has a Start" was a primary reason why it rose to excellence. A band shouldn't strive for an anthemic sound if it lacks the words for something to say.

Behind Smith, the group was exceptional. As Chris Urbanowicz led the battery of careening guitars that filled the mid-range, drummer Ed Lay found clever ways to tee up the dynamics and drive the band with power and taste. Smith was responsible for the piano parts, which add a different color to the band sound as in "Push Your Head Toward the Air" and "A Thousand Pieces." Bassist Russell Leetch handled his dual roles: stepping into the mid-range when the opportunity opened and yet held down the bottom with authority. There were moments in the magnificent "The Racing Rats" in which Lay, Leetch and Smith's piano locked in so thoroughly that the effect was exhilarating.

Perhaps aware that others could do as well with the kind of post-punk rock of "An End Has a Start," the members of Editors began to change their sound on the follow-up, "In This Light and On This Evening," which moved the guitars into a secondary role. Urbanowicz left the band before they recorded their fourth album, "The Weight of Your Love," released in 2013.

Rightfully so, "An End Has a Start" was an unqualified success. It attained platinum status in the U.K. (In the U.K., that's 300,000 units sold.) The opening track, "Smokers Outside the Hospital," was a top-10 hit single at home. The group was nominated for a Brit Award for Best British Group, which was won by Arctic Monkeys. "An End Has a Start" established Editors as a band of merit and may have well reordered the list of the greatest post-punk albums.

Veckatimest

Grizzly Bear | *2009*

An experimental work rich in unexpected airy arrangements and extended instrumental passages

In 2005, singer and guitarist Daniel Rossen signed on to Grizzly Bear, once a project of Ed Droste, who was joined on the group's early recordings by drummer Christopher Bear and bassist/multi-instrumentalist Chris Taylor. The Brooklyn-based quartet recorded "Yellow House," a solid album of unconventional rock and off-kilter chamber pop with bright vocal arrangements. After opening for Radiohead on tour — Jonny Greenwood is said to have told an audience that Grizzly Bear was his favorite band — the group settled in to write and record "Veckatimest." It's a masterpiece.

On their first collaborative recording — for "Yellow House," Droste and Rossen presented their band mates with almost-completed compositions — "Veckatimest" has a force and cohesiveness absent from earlier albums released under the Grizzly Bear name. And yet it's an experimental work rich in unexpected airy arrangements with extended instrumental passages; curiously stacked vocal harmonies and choral singing (by the band and a youth chorus); and string arrangements by Nico Muhly. Attitude and atmosphere are a primary source of communication, as much as fuzzy guitars, darting percussion, cellos and reeds, and soaring voices. From the early '60s Brill Building vibe of "Cheerleader" to the jarring clattering of "I Live With You," the song structures discard the standard rock format in favor of a freer presentation. With its melancholic mood and embrace of melodrama, "Veckatimest" struck a balance between accessible and challenging.

As if an unconventional recording needed an unconventional release, bits of "Veckatimest" were presented to audiences before it was available via commercial outlets: Grizzly Bear played tracks from the album on TV's "Late Show with David Letterman," "Late Night with Conan O'Brien" and, as the official street date drew near, "Later…with Jools Holland." The band executed the knotty arrangements and vocal harmonies with aplomb in live settings.

Grizzly Bear toured aggressively behind "Veckatimest," which, by the way, takes its name from a small Massachusetts island. The album sold well, reaching the number-one slot in the Billboard chart that tracks albums on independent labels. It found a champion in the late Philip Seymour Hoffman, who featured several tracks from the disc in his solo effort as a film director, "Jack Goes Boating," released in 2010.

Grizzly Bear went on hiatus after the "Veckatimest" tour, and Taylor and Rossen released solo albums. The band reunited and after a tentative start, rallied to record "Shields," another excellent album that was issued in September 2012. The "Shields" tour concluded in January 2014 with a performance at the Sydney Opera House.

Given the quality of "Shields," it's premature to declare "Veckatimest" the best album Grizzly Bear will make: their talent is vast, as is their desire to push beyond what they've done before without abandoning their essence. Warm and intelligent, "Veckatimest" was often beautiful and never less than captivating, and it remains a wonder, as fresh and revealing today as it was when it was issued.

Standing At The Sky's Edge

Richard Hawley | *2012*

Love, rage and guitars inspired a superb album.

After five full-length studio albums of lush ballads that recalled Roy Orbison and mid-'60s British orchestral pop, Richard Hawley decided to nudge romance to the side and use his guitar and band to communicate his growing anger. The resulting album, the stunning "Standing at the Sky's Edge," for the most part placed his rich voice amid a squall of powerful electric guitars and synthesizers — a perfect accompaniment to his lyrical themes.

Though he was better known for his voice and compositions, Hawley already had a reputation as a guitarist prior to "Standing at the Sky's Edge," which was released in 2012. (He's pictured on the cover of his 2007 album "Lady's Bridge" with a big-bodied Gretsch guitar resting on his thigh.) A resident of Sheffield, a city in central England, he played briefly with Pulp and contributed to albums by All Saints, Elbow and Nancy Sinatra, among others, and accompanied himself on all his discs. The death of his friend Tim McCall, a Sheffield guitarist, drove him back to the instrument they both loved.

Each of Hawley's albums was inspired by Sheffield — several titles refer to locations in the city — and "Standing at the Sky's Edge" was too, though not a source of misty memory and nostalgia. The son and grandson of steelworkers, Hawley was irked — perhaps disgusted is a better word — by the ongoing gentrification of Sheffield following an influx of white-collar jobs in finance, information technology, tourism and a variety of services.

Following McCall's death, Hawley was upset further when a newly elected government announced that it wanted to sell the woodlands where he walked with his grandfather as a child and would allow his dogs to roam. He directed his emotions into a successful campaign to block the sale — and into "Standing at the Sky's Edge."

The album opened with the distant stirring of sound that drew nearer until it exploded into "She Brings the Sunlight." Hawley's warm, steady voice was out front, but not by much and the music, including his nasty, squealing guitar solo, threatened to engulf him. Love was tossed aside in the title track: it was about murder and despair; his characters were "sliding down the razor's edge," their lives "slowly sinking." Again, a patient underpinning gave way to a furious roar. By the time "Down in the Woods" arrived, Hawley was into full-blast rock with drummer Dean Beresford and bassist Colin Elliot driving the group behind and around him.

Reminiscent of Hawley's earlier recordings, a stretch of lovely ballads provided a respite. Dripping with ardor and tenderness, "Don't Stare at the Sun" was a masterpiece that showcased his voice and approach to songwriting. A threatening undercurrent informed "The Wood Colliers Grave," and fury returned with "Leave Your Body Behind You," as a ghostly chorus joined Hawley to repeat the title. "Before" concluded the disk with stately ferocity that faded into a dewy beauty.

"Standing at the Sky's Edge" was nominated for a Mercury Prize. It was Hawley's second opportunity for the prize: in 2006, his album "Coles Corner" was a nominee and when it didn't win, Alex Turner of the Arctic Monkeys, a Sheffield band that won the award, said: "Someone call 999. Richard Hawley's been robbed." "Standing at the Sky's Edge" didn't win either. But it is a superb album, one that brought Hawley's many gifts into focus and enhanced his reputation for excellence.

Scar

Joe Henry | *2001*

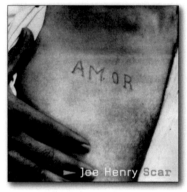

Moments of muted beauty characterized the heart of "Scar."

For "Scar," singer-songwriter Joe Henry veered from the kind of smart, offbeat alt-country of his previous seven albums. He kept the "smart" and the "offbeat;" what he added was jazz and the blues. The result: an aural kaleidoscope in grays and indigo; a song dedicated to Richard Pryor; a guest appearance by Ornette Coleman; and unforgettably captivating music by an artist who at that point was probably best known as Madonna's brother-in-law.

On "Scar," Henry surrounded himself with a core band that included Brian Blade on drums, Meshell Ndegeocello and David Pilch on bass, and Marc Ribot on guitar; Henry played guitars, keyboards and percussion. He also co-produced along with Craig Street, who had developed a style that surrounded intriguing vocalists with unexpected arrangements and unusual soundscapes. For his part, Ribot was reinventing the electric guitar, and much as he did when working with Tom Waits, his refined noise lent the music an exhilarating dimension.

The album opened with "Richard Pryor Addresses a Tearful Nation," a melancholy dirge that was all but formless. As if adding a splash of a brighter blue to the music, Coleman's solo enlivened the environment as Henry sang "Love me like you're lying, let me feel you near/Remember me for trying and excuse me while I disappear," the last phrase copped from the jazz standard "Angel Eyes." The bonus track version of "Scar" concluded with a reprise of "Pryor" where Coleman soloed over ghostly, atmospheric guitar by Ribot and distant industrial sounds.

The band entered like a drowsy combo behind a bloated stripper on the tango "Stop," which may be Henry's best-known song. Madonna recorded it as "Don't Tell Me" on her album, "Music." (Henry married her sister, Melanie Ciccone, in 1987.) His version has a hint of desperation that suits the lyric.

M oments of muted beauty characterized the heart of "Scar." "Mean Flower," "Lock and Key" — with the line "I wonder how you turned out the stars" — and "Cold Enough to Cross" are lovely ballads, the latter two featuring Henry on piano. Ribot played a delicate solo on nylon-string guitar on "Struck." In "Rough and Tumble," Henry rode a nice groove by the rhythm section sparked by Blade's cymbal work.

Henry enjoyed deploying in his songs familiar public figures in unfamiliar settings or as a reference point. On "Scar," it was also Edgar Bergen, the ventriloquist, and Nico, the singer with the Velvet Underground. "Edgar Bergen" was in the form of a letter: "Dear Marion" opened the tune followed by "Baby knows I love to cry…I just sit up on her knee and wait for the whole world to change." Steven Barber wrote the dizzying string charts. The jazzy instrumental "Nico Lost One Small Buddha" was a showcase for Ribot's wah-wah heavy guitar.

Henry's career soared after "Scar," both as a solo artist and a producer. He produced albums by artists as varied as Solomon Burke, Ani DiFranco, Salif Keita, Bettye LaVette, Meshell Ndegeocello and Allen Toussaint, among others. Henry's released five albums since "Scar," including "Blood from Stars," a 2009 release that found him exploring New Orleans and roguish blues with Ribot and a skilled band in tune with Henry's vibe.

Thus, "Scar" was a milestone in Henry's career: a summit after his early work and a springboard for what followed and may yet come.

The Blueprint

Jay Z | *2001*

Hip hop as part of the continuum of American R&B and soul

"The Blueprint," Jay Z's sixth album, not only confirmed his skills as an executive producer and rapper, it presented hip hop as part of the continuum of American R&B and soul.

"The Blueprint" continued a creative spurt that began with Jay Z's debut album, "Reasonable Doubt," which was released in 1996. But his 2000 album "The Dynasty: Roc La Familia" was more a showcase of rappers signed to his Roc-A-Fella Records, and it brought producer Kanye West into the label's fold. The arrival of West, as well as the duo the Neptunes — Pharrell Williams and Chad Hugo — and Bink and Just Blaze, introduced new sounds to Jay Z's arsenal on "The Dynasty," which carried over to "The Blueprint."

It's been reported that Jay Z wrote the lyrics to "The Blueprint" in just two days, and the album was recorded in two weeks. In this case, haste did not harm quality. Only Eminem was a prominent guest voice. He appeared as a counterpoint on "Renegade," a track he produced that rose from a piano intro and rode on bass notes played in upper range. Timbaland, who collaborated with Jay Z on several earlier albums, produced one track, "Hola' Hovito."

Tracks produced by Bink and Just Blaze favored classic soul's melodramatic backdrops. The latter's "Girls, Girls, Girls" contained a sample from a track by Tom Brock, an associate of Barry White, and the broken-love tune "Song Cry" draws from Bobby Glenn's "Sounds Like A Song," which featured both harp and blues piano. Bink's "The Ruler's Game," which kicked off the album, used swirling strings and brass, and his "U Don't Know" sampled Bobby Byrd's "I Need Help."

West positioned his borrowed soul and rock tracks in stark relief. "Never Change" hopped on David Ruffin's "Common Man" while "Heart of the City (Ain't No Love)" was a virtual tribute to Bobby Blue Bland's "Ain't No Love in the Heart of the City." In "Takeover," Jay Z rapped around treated samples from the Doors' "Five to One." Snippets from the Jackson 5's "I Want You Back" floated in the background of "Izzo (H.O.V.A.)."

With his rapid-fire lyrics, Jay Z the rapper was on his game on "The Blueprint," whether he was exhorting about the high life, street life or his love life. "I sell ice in the winter/I sell fire in hell/I'm a hustler, baby, I'll sell water to a well," he rapped in "U Don't Know." At the time, other rappers were taking verbal shots at Jay Z and here he chose to respond. "No, you're not on my level/Get your brakes tweaked/I sold what your whole album sold in my first week" was his retort to Mobb Deep and Nas's attacks. "Yeah, you shinin' but the only thing you're leavin' out: You're a candle in the sun," he raps in "Hola' Hovito."

Though the album was released on September 11, 2001, "The Blueprint" sold at a pace comparable to other Jay Z albums, achieving and then exceeding double-platinum status — that is, more than two million sold. (It may be at the three-million mark by now.) Along with "Reasonable Doubt" and "The Black Album," issued in 2006, "The Blueprint" is considered the finest album by the genre's finest rapper. With its embrace of classic soul music, it illustrates how Jay Z and his producers found inspiration in rich, traditional American music.

I Never Heard You Knockin'

Malcolm Holcombe | *2005*

A stark look at life's hard-learned lessons

By the time Malcolm Holcombe recorded "I Never Heard You Knockin'," life had kicked him around hard and often.

Starting out in 1976, the singer-songwriter played his way around Asheville, North Carolina, and Florida's Gulf Coast before taking a chance on Nashville in '90. It didn't work out for him in Music City, and drugs and drinking intervened. He worked menial jobs and pulled himself together enough to record a couple of albums. A son died at an early age.

He returned to Asheville, which isn't far from his hometown of Weaverville, to record "I Heard You Knockin'," a remarkable document of his hardscrabble life and the aural equivalent of found art.

Backed only by his guitar, the album recalled Holcombe's live shows during which he unleashed his growling howl of a voice to sing deeply affecting lyrics while finger-picking gently or attacking the wood and strings. At his best, Holcombe brought the listener in close and his stories landed powerfully on the heart and mind.

In his tales on "I Never Heard You Knockin'," Holcombe weaved between past and present, as happens when memories are pulled forward. He employed metaphor and reportage. "That big ol' front door had steel from side to side/It never had a key/Windows painted shut, didn't matter anyhow," he sang in the title track. In "This Town Knows Me," he was more direct: "This town knows me lyin' on my face/Broken gutters and cussin' the rain." He sang the words with barely contained rage.

Holcombe was at his most disarming when he revealed his tender side. In "Mama Told Me So," he addressed his fear of aging alone. "Who's gonna love me when I'm old?" he sang. "You're the only one who's ever loved me true and kind. I cover my ears to the pain of you leaving me behind." He appreciated keenly the simple things. "Layin' rock, drivin' a nail, drivin' a truck, deliverin' mail/Jesus is there and he never fails when I'm doin' my job... Thank you, lord sweet lord, for my job."

But Holcombe always seemed aware of the looming dark side. "Been knocked down flat all over this place," he sang, his throat full of gravel, in "For the Love." "Dyin' in my grave that I dug myself. I'm gonna sing like a slave 'cause there's nothing left."

"I Never Heard You Knockin'" gave Holcombe a well-deserved moment the spotlight , but he wasn't, and still isn't, the kind of artist who has an instinct for commercial success. He followed it with "Gamblin' House," which softened some of the raw emotion of its predecessor. But in 2015, he released "The RCA Sessions," a 16-song set in which he was backed by a sweet country quartet whose performance contrasted with Holcombe's growling, gargly delivery — and that disparity worked to a compelling effect, sort of like a beautiful frame around a disturbing painting. He followed it with a tour of Western Europe and the U.S.

As for "I Never Heard You Knockin'," it was a stark look at life's hard-learned lessons set to songs delivered with intensity by an artist who tapped into a deep vein of truth.

Donuts

J Dilla | *2006*

In 43 minutes, the past, present and future of several American popular music forms

"Donuts" was released three days after J Dilla's death at age 32. Suffering from lupus and the rare blood disease thrombotic thrombocytopenic purpura or TTP, J Dilla knew he was quite ill when he recorded "Donuts": he created almost all of its tracks while hospitalized. Only one track exceeded two minutes; many clocked in about 90 seconds. But in the album's 43 minutes of music, we heard the past, present and future of several American popular music forms.

Born James Dewitt Yancey in Detroit, J Dilla was surrounded by music from birth. His mother, Maureen Yancey, studied opera and sang in her church choir; his father, Beverly Dewitt Yancey, was a jazz bassist. He began making notable beats while in high school, working in a studio he put together in the family basement. He formed Slum Village, a hip hop trio, and his reputation as a producer flourished.

Under the guise of The Ummah, a production trio that included Q-Tip and Ali Shaheed Muhammad of A Tribe Called Quest, Dilla participated in the making or remixing of hits by Janet and Michael Jackson, Jamiroquai and Busta Rhymes, among others. With J Dilla on hand, A Tribe Called Quest, which had embraced jazz as part of its sound since its first album, unwound a bit, toyed with the downbeat and swung with the rhythm.

Along with D'Angelo, James Poyser, Ahmir "Questlove" Thompson and others, Dilla was a founding member of the

Soulquarians, which had a hand in the production of albums by Erykah Badu, Common and Talib Kweli. His debut solo album "Welcome 2 Detroit," released in 2001, featured tracks influenced by hip hop, jazz, bossa nova and prog rock.

Legend has it Dilla made "Donuts" using a digital sampler and a turntable that spun 45s. But the album transcended technology, however limited, and it was Dilla's feel for rhythm, encyclopedic knowledge of all forms of popular music and lack of bias that gave it its timeless, magical glow.

Dilla's gleeful, audacious crosscutting approach to production defines "Donuts," named for his favorite snack. In "Workinonit," he blended samples from Beastie Boys, Malcolm McLaren, Mantronix, Raymond Scott, Sweet Charles Sherrell and 10cc, all of which rode on a insistent drum pattern that held together what could have been chaos. "Waves" was a nod toward a future of groove-based electronic dance music while "Stop!" had at its heart a Dionne Warwick ballad that Dilla overloaded with big beats from a Jadakiss track.

There was a touch of the subversive at work on "Donuts." In "People," he used the percussion and chanting of the Eddie Kendricks song "My People... Hold On" and married it to sounds from a Bollywood track, a blast of horns, and bone-crushing beats by Run-D.M.C. A tribute to old-school soul, "Glazed" chopped and reassembled horns from a Jerry Butler-Gene Chandler track and tossed in bits from songs by Lou Rawls and the Temptations. As a tribute to his hometown, Dilla sampled Motown tracks by the Jackson 5, Kendricks, the Temptations, the Undisputed Truth and Stevie Wonder — the joyous "The Twister (Huh, What)" jumps off Wonder's "For Once in My Life."

Countless artists have incorporate Dilla's approach to sound into their music, including Robert Glasper and Greg Osby. Whether Dilla's openness to every kind of music, regardless of its origins, was a reflection of, or an inspiration for, the all-embracing approach we see among some of today's young musicians may be hard to discern. But his spirit is alive whenever a music fan, regardless of age or predisposition, opens his mind to something new and savors its value.

That Lonesome Song

Jamey Johnson | *2008*

A perfect marriage of compositions, singer and performance

A reasonable reaction to the first exposure to Jamey Johnson's "That Lonesome Song": I didn't know they made country albums like that anymore.

Truth is, they don't, at least not often enough. "That Lonesome Song," was a tumbledown chronicle of the hard way to recover a life and career. We heard in Johnson's growl echoes of Merle Haggard and Waylon Jennings and George Jones when they too were down and desperate.

Born in 1975 and raised in Montgomery, Alabama, the town where Hank Williams is buried, Johnson left college to join the Marine Reserves, where he served stateside for eight years. In 2000, he relocated to Nashville, elbowing his way into the music scene by singing demos. His voice brought him the attention of producers, as well as singers like Trace Adkins, Big & Rich and Gretchen Wilson. Working odd jobs and construction, he financed and self-released his debut album, "They Call Me Country."

Johnson entered the Nashville machine, signing with a subsidiary of Sony Music. He released "The Dollar," his major-label debut that included a contribution from Jones. It doesn't work: the band sounded generic, and Johnson seemed to be pulling back from digging down and letting loose. Dropped by the label, he retreated and sold songs he co-wrote to Adkins, Joe Nichols and George Strait.

As if reborn, Johnson returned with "That Lonesome

Song," a perfect marriage of compositions, singer and performance that Johnson released himself in digital form in '07. A declaration of freedom from the Nashville's pop-country system, it opened with a metaphor: Johnson leaving prison; "Mr. Johnson, as of now you're free to do whatever you want to do," the jailer told him. By the time the album concluded with "Between Jennings and Jones," Johnson had revealed what had gone wrong and how he started to set things right.

The prettification that muted "The Dollar" was swept aside by Johnson and producer Dave Cobb. The band, which also produced several tracks, was loose and limber. Punctuating cluck-pluck guitar added color, as did the pedal steel, played by Cowboy Eddie Long and former Jennings sideman Robbie Turner. Swamp funk, outlaw country and traditional country were conveyed with affecting ease.

Largely inspired by autobiography, the writing was superb, particularly the ballads like "Angel," a tale of divorce, and "Stars in Alabama," by Johnson and Teddy Gentry. Love gone astray fuels "Mary Go Round," the tale of a woman who "takes her heartache to town." Though the "High Cost of Living" drew on a familiar Nashville songwriting technique of flipping a phrase — "The high cost of living ain't nothing like the cost of living high" — it worked because of the delivery of Johnson and the band.

Written with Lee Thomas Miller and James Otto, "In Color" told of a man and his grandfather as they revisited hard times. It became Johnson's first big hit, winning Song of the Year awards from the Academy of Country Music and Country Music Association. Two songs associated with Jennings — Dickey Lee and Bob McDill's "The Door is Always Open" and Allen Reynolds' miraculous "Dreaming My Dreams with You" — sat perfectly with the original material.

His career on a new path, in 2010 Johnson released "The Guitar Song," which reached the top slot on Billboard's country-album charts. Two years later, his Hank Cochran tribute "Living for a Song" found him in a duet setting with Haggard, Emmylou Harris, Alison Krauss, Ray Price, Willie Nelson and others. In late 2014, he released a Christmas-themed EP.

As for "That Lonesome Song": thus far, it's the best country album of the 21st century.

Naturally

Sharon Jones & the Dap-Kings | *2005*

On "Naturally" Sharon Jones, a fiery singer of the classic-soul school, and composer-bandleader Bosco Mann (the alias of bassist Gabriel Roth) gave the Dap-Kings a snap that transcended era even as they looked back. As Ms. Jones said, "There ain't nothing retro about me. We're not hopping on anybody's band wagon." Recorded at the House of Soul, the Dap-King's analogue studio in Brooklyn, "Naturally" put the band on its path to international success.

On "Naturally," Jones dug in amid a whirlwind of funk.

The Dap-Kings were formed in 2000. Jones quit a successful wedding band to travel with the Dap-Kings to a 2001 residency at a club in Barcelona. The group's debut album, "Dap Dippin' with Sharon Jones & the Dap-Kings" was released officially in 2002 — copies had leaked out before then. The Dap-Kings shifted lineups prior to the "Naturally" sessions, which featured Leon Michels on baritone sax, Neal Sugarman on tenor sax and Binky Griptite on guitar, among others. Roth's relentless bass was at the heart of many arrangements and Homer Steinweiss — known as Funky Foot — provided seriously tasty drive.

So "Naturally," Jones dug in amid a whirlwind of funk. In "Your Thing is a Drag," Roth put down a snappy bass line that percussionist Fernando Velez punctuated on congas. The horns and crisp guitar chords teed up the '60s James Brown-like "My Man is a Mean Man." "How Long Do I Have to Wait for You?" featured a watery guitar riff and a pattern on the drums that emphasized the kick, allowing Roth to lock in to make the bottom extra thick. Trumpeter David Guy stepped out for a brief, effective solo.

Jones was the centerpiece, singing with verve and personality. "Naturally" was home to heartbreak songs, leave-me-be songs, silly and sexy songs, and a funk cover of "This Land is Your Land": she worked them all with smoky ease. But she was far from the album's lone bright spot. The horns' unison playing provided texture, muscle and charm. At times, they were out front as prominently as was Jones. As dynamic as she was, the horns made the Dap-Kings something special.

Among the magic moments on "Naturally" was a great soul ballad written by Roth and sung by Jones and Lee Fields. It's a story song: Fields' car was stolen, so he turned up at Jones' doorstep looking for a place to stay. They quarreled — Jones was sharp-tongued as Fields connived — and negotiations began. Did she let him come inside? Therein rested the tale.

With "Naturally," the Dap-Kings' reputation blossomed. Guitarist Thomas Brenneck, Griptite, Roth, Steinweiss and Sugarman were recruited by Mark Ronson to contribute to Amy Winehouse's breakout "Back to Black." The band followed "Naturally" with three albums including 2014's "Give the People What They Want," which marked Jones' return after a battle with cancer. The Dap-Kings now headline concerts and play the main stage at festivals, bringing traditional soul and funk to new audiences in the U.S. and overseas. They've fulfilled the promise they demonstrated on "Naturally" and continue to honor their forbearers with their work.

Go

Jónsi | *2010*

A sunny cry of freedom and an expression of absolute joy

In January 2010, Sigur Rós, one of the world's great bands, announced that it was going on hiatus after releasing five albums of majestic music. As the Reykjavik-based quartet came to their decision to rest, lead singer Jónsi set to work on a solo album.

Released four months after the band's announcement, "Go" was a work that found no precedent in the Sigur Rós catalogue. Whereas the group sound, influenced by contemporary classical music and prog rock, emphasized suspense, mystery and grandeur, "Go" was at times giddy and an expression of absolute joy. It was as if Jónsi, who often seemed impenetrable as he stood before Sigur Rós and sang in Icelandic or an invented language dubbed Hopelandic, had decided to reveal the flip side of his personality. The result was as much a shock as it was a delight.

Jónsi, whose full name is Jón Þór Birgisson, recorded "Go" in Reykjavik and Bridgeport, Connecticut during the summer of 2009. Perhaps coincidentally, the first track Jónsi issued — "Boy Lilikoi," via his website prior to the album's official release — was a sunny cry of freedom. Over wind chimes, clattering percussion and strings arranged by Nico Muhly, Jónsi sang in a sweet falsetto, "Wild boy, wild beam, you burn so bright," adding in what may have been an allusion to tension within Sigur Rós: "One day you're out, you give up the fight, you slow heart rate down." The song was inspired by the singer-composer's visit to Hawaii, which has a different sort of beauty than his somber-sky homeland.

"Boy Lilikoi" proved an accurate harbinger of the full album, which opens with "Go Do," another burst of bliss. "You should always know that we can do anything," sang Jónsi, accompanied by flutes and sizzling cymbals. "Tie strings to clouds. Make your own lake/Let it flow."

His voice soared on the ballads: Muhly's gorgeous strings lifted him on "Tornado," which had the right touch of melodrama in its underpinning. In the magnificent "Kolnidur," Jónsi sang in the lower register of his range, percussion and string jabbing and prodding him as the music reached a crescendo. (Though he delivered "Kolnidur" in Icelandic, the power of the emotion communicated clearly.) In "Grow Will Tall," he sang: "You'll know when's time to go on/You'll really want to grow and grow till tall." As if addressing detractors, he added: "They all, in the end, will fall."

Jónsi toured behind "Go," with a talented group capable of transmitting the album's gentleness and joy. The stage was dressed as if it were a wildlife-rich forest with the singer as a pan in its midst, toy pianos, xylophones, and drums and cymbals of all sizes around him. A CD and DVD of the "Go" live performance was released in 2011, as was a film of Jónsi playing acoustic versions of the album's songs.

Afterward, he returned to Sigur Rós. When we met in Reykjavik, he told me, "It was like coming home to see the guys again. It felt natural." Sigur Rós returned to their studio. They've since issued two studio albums, including "Kveikur" in 2013. Jónsi continues to work outside the mother ship: he wrote and performed the music for the soundtracks for the Cameron Crowe films "We Bought A Zoo" and, with his partner Alex Somers, "Aloha." Jónsi also contributed songs to the soundtrack for "How to Train Your Dragon 2."

With "Go," Jónsi demonstrated that an artist can use the freedom of independence to reveal himself and create a jubilant work, one that's imbued with a touch of magic.

PS_BX04371570

CreateSpace
7290 Investment Drive Suite B
North Charleston, SC 29418

Question About Your Order?
Log in to your account at www.createspace.com and "Contact
Support."

11/10/2015 04:11:25 PM
Order ID: 105772991

Qty.	Item
	IN THIS SHIPMENT
9	Catching Up 151537615X

Songs in A Minor

Alicia Keys | *2001*

At age 20, Keys displayed technical virtuosity and steely self-assurance.

It's rare that an artist arrives as fully formed as did Alicia Keys on her debut album, "Songs in A Minor." At 20 years old, Keys displayed maturity as a singer, pianist, composer and arranger as she blended contemporary sounds with soul, pop, jazz, gospel and classical music.

With the guidance of Clive Davis, who had nurtured the careers of Aretha Franklin, Whitney Houston, Patti Smith, Dionne Warwick and many others, "Songs in A Minor" was launched with a smart, targeted strategy. "Girlfriend" was issued as a single to urban-music radio, on the bet that the hip-hop audience would dig the edgy rhythms and rhymes set to staccato chords and tidy flourishes on piano. A video for the stirring soul ballad "Fallin'" was leaked to MTV.

When "Songs in A Minor" was released, it turned out that the two early tracks foreshadowed "Songs in A Minor" without revealing the breadth of Keys' talent or the album's consistency. From the opening moments, Keys declared what followed would be predicated on her voice, piano and self-confidence as an artist. (Keys opened the album by introducing herself over a Beethoven piano sonata set to hip-hop beats.) But her steely self-assurance was juxtaposed with the subject of several songs, including "Girlfriend" and "Fallin'": love is a battlefield; and heartache hurts deeply when it strikes.

Yet on "Jane Doe," the defiant Keys emerged: no one was going to steal her man. And in "Goodbye," with its stuttering synth percussion, she struggled with a choice of whether to let a good man go. When romance works, asserted the young singer, it's wonderful: "Never Felt This Way," featuring Keys and her piano, was a pledge of love; and it folded into "Butterflyz," in which an acoustic guitar joined the quiet, intense environment. Love , it said, was a transcendent joy.

For the most part, Keys confined herself to the mid tempo and kept experimentation at a minimum. Strings gave "Troubles" its dark underpinning. "Rock Wit U" featured a long orchestral intro with driving drums and a wet wah-wah guitar, and Keys entered at the bottom of vocal register; later, she doubled her voice by singing an octave above the entry point. "The Life" also jumped off with a long, swirling intro, this time featuring Latin percussion. "How Come You Don't Call Me," written by Prince, was delivered as a marriage of gospel and soul.

"Fallin'," which featured a feisty yet heart-tugging vocal by Keys and was a major hit, is often referred to as Keys' greatest moment on "Songs in A Minor." But as fine as it was, it didn't quite rise to level of the extraordinary "A Woman's Worth." Composed by Keys and Erika Rose, the song was a declaration: "You will lose if you chose to refuse to put her first/She will and she can find a man who knows her worth." Keys' approach to the vocal was perfection: while laying down the challenge, at the same time she communicated her desire for what she demanded. Keys overdubbed her voice to form a choir that delivered the punch: "A real man just can't deny a woman's worth."

"Songs in A Minor" went on to capture five Grammys and sell more than 12 million copies worldwide. It established Keys as an artist of significant promise, which she's fulfilled with four subsequent albums and international tours, including a series of solo shows to commemorate the 10th anniversary of her debut's release. She remains a major star to this day, deservedly so.

A Church
That Fits Our Needs

Lost in the Trees | *2012*

Facing
tragedy
with beauty
and art
on his side

In 2006, Ari Picker nominated his mom, the artist Karen Shelton, to be celebrated on CBS's "The Early Show." Praising her spirit, he described how she had endured a challenging life: the death of twin girls born prematurely; an abusive relationship; and then breast cancer, at a time when she was without insurance. CBS granted Picker's wish, giving Shelton a trip from North Carolina to New York for a fashion makeover, with Glamour magazine and Macy's among those who pitched in. An art supplier donated a $2,500 gift certificate and a Soho gallery promised to show her work at a reception.

Of her son, who was studying at the Berklee School of Music, Shelton told CBS, "He does magic for me."

Three years later, Shelton committed suicide. Picker and his chamber-rock band Lost in the Trees paid homage to her with a remarkable album, "A Church That Fits Our Needs."

It works for several reasons. One is Picker's thoughtful and sensitive portrayal of his mother and his reaction to the news of her death. On Lost in the Trees' previous album, "All Alone in an Empty House," Picker wrote of his parents' rancorous relationship, so he had already established that he wouldn't veer from tackling difficult subjects close to his heart. But "A Church That Fits Our Needs" required special care. Picker wanted to ensure Shelton was memorialized properly and that her suicide did not dominate the view of her life.

Picker made clear he understood the depth of his mother's pain. "I heard you weep through walls," he wrote in "Red." "Golden Eyelids" reviews, or re-contextualizes, her reaction to her cancer and the loss of her twin girls. In the aftermath of Shelton's death, the narrative shifts; in "Icy River," Picker wrote: "Don't you ever dare think she was weak-hearted/She led me to the woods where our church was started/Like a ribbon of silver, I poured her body in the river."

Picker churns through a tumult of emotions and arrives at acceptance in "An Artist's Song": "You walked through this horrid life/But you got to sing before you closed your eyes.../A fearful song played by trumpets for my heart."

Another reason "A Church That Fits Our Needs" resonates so thoroughly is Picker's inventive arrangements, largely for folk guitar, percussion, a string ensemble and his sweet, reedy voice. He studied composition at Berklee and his sympathetic orchestrations are perfectly suited to the sentiment of the lyric: the clarity of his love for his mother outweighs his confusion over his sudden loss.

Picker said he was compelled to pay tribute to his mother. "It would be cheating her not to do so," he told me in '12. "I was raised by an artist mother. I learned you have art on your side."

He added, "I was spinning the tragedy in a positive light and embracing the memories of my mom. There are beautiful angelic things about her."

Lost in the Trees toured widely behind "A Church That Fits Our Needs," which was acclaimed critically. In 2014, the group released "Past Life," another work of quiet intensity that profited from a lean sound and a new approach to percussion. The new album portrayed, indirectly, that Picker had moved on, at least in his art. He did so having enriching our appreciation not only of his mother, but the anguish endured by the battered and depressed, with a masterpiece in "A Church That Fits Our Needs."

Hurry Up, We're Dreaming

M83 | *2011*

Prog rock met electronica in a soundtrack to an imaginary movie.

When Anthony Gonzalez, who records and performs as M83, set out to craft his sixth album, he had in mind an ambitious rock-meets-electronic music project, one with the scope of earlier recordings by Genesis in its Peter Gabriel period, Gorillaz, Pink Floyd, Sigur Rós and Smashing Pumpkins. He achieved it with "Hurry Up, We're Dreaming."

It was an epic work of power and grandeur. Throughout the course of its 22 tracks, it visited many forms of contemporary rock, always with purpose but never with self-consciousness. It announced its intention with its prog-rock overture that bled into an impressive stretch of five songs that serve as a declaration of Gonzalez's aspiration and influences. In "Midnight City," gunfire drumming ripped through the layers of synthesizers by Gonzalez and Justin Meldal-Johnsen (who worked with Air, Beck and Nine Inch Nails) that floated beneath Gonzalez's vocal and an alto-sax solo by James King of Fitz and the Tantrums. "Reunion" rose from guitar power chords and a driving, New Wavy pattern on the high-hat cymbals. Following the synth-strings interlude "Where the Boats Go," "Wait" invoked Pink Floyd during its "Dark Side of the Moon" period, intentionally so, Gonzalez said. "Raconte-Moi Une Histoire," which translates to "Tell Me a Story," was a fairy tale in which, over popcorn synths, a young girl told the saga of a magic frog.

M83 began in Antibes, France, in 2001 as a do-it-yourself project for Gonzalez and his musical partner, Nicolas Fromageau. They made their first two albums before Fromageau departed. Gonzalez hired musicians and completed the third M83 disk, "Before the Dawn Heals Us."

While writing and recording at his home studio "Digital Shades, Vol. 1," an album of ambient music, Gonzalez remixed tracks by Bloc Party, Depeche Mode, Goldfrapp and others. With his band, he developed his stagecraft by opening on tour for Depeche Mode, the Killers and the Kings of Leon. After witnessing arena-rock acts up close, Gonzalez refined his goals and relocated to Los Angeles to do a large-scale work, his growing ambition influenced in part by the score he composed for Gilles Marchand's 2010 film "L'autre Monde." Gonzalez said "Hurry Up, We're Dreaming" was "written like a soundtrack to imaginary movie."

After such a powerful opening, "Hurry Up and Dreaming" was bound to drop off, but it didn't, at least not steeply. The first disc concluded with four melancholy mid-tempo ballads, including "Soon, My Friend," in which layers of voices rose above a folk guitar that gave way to an orchestra. The mood continued with the opening of side two, but was blasted to dust by "New Map," a roaring rocker. Later, "Steve McQueen" served as a declaration of power and self-realization: "Nothing can hurt me today...There's a magic inside just waiting to burst out." In the finale, "Outro," the singer declared "I am the king of my own land." The album concludes with a piano chord that all but whispers "Amen."

In the years since, Gonzalez composed two film scores, including one for the Joseph Kosinski film "Oblivion." A new M83 song, "I Need You," appeared in "Divergent," the Neil Burger film released in 2014, and Gonzalez's "Holes in the Sky" was featured in the 2015 follow-up film "Insurgent."

As for "Hurry Up, We're Dreaming," it's M83 best-selling album thus far, its sales boosted by a lengthy tour that included appearances at the Coachella Music & Arts Festival and other major events in the U.S. and overseas. The Wall Street Journal and Filter named it their Album of the Year, and eMusic, Paste, Pitchfork and Popmatters included it on their Top 10 lists for 2011.

It remains a savory marvel of fulfilled ambition by an artist still emerging as a composer and who may very well be considered a visionary.

Heligoland

Massive Attack | *2010*

The best work by a collective that never made the same album twice

Fans of Massive Attack, Robert Del Naja and Grant Marshall's trip-hop collective, might argue that "Blue Lines," their 1991 debut album, is their best work. Others might tout "Mezzanine," their '98 release. They're both superb recordings, and only somewhat alike. "Blue Lines" is down-tempo house seasoned with jazz and soul; "Mezzanine" dark and brooding to the point of threatening. Both feature an excellent collection of vocalists: Shara Nelson and Tricky on the former, Cocteau Twins' Elizabeth Fraser on the latter, and reggae singer Horace Andy on both.

But "Heligoland" is Massive Attack's greatest album. It featured a superior marriage of compositions and arrangements, musicianship and vocalists. It also provided the raw material for an extraordinary live show that pointed to the band's intent — to create a seamless fusion of experimental electronica and live improvisational music in a rock setting.

To its credit, Massive Attack never made the same album twice; that is, they went in search of new modes of expression as soon as an album was completed, at times pressing on despite internal strife. Though "Mezzanine" sold some four million copies and reached the top spot on the charts in the U.K. — their home country; they're based in Bristol — Marshall withdrew during the recording of the follow-up, "The 100th Window." Del Naja and producer Neil Davidge put together "The 100th Window" with Sinéad O'Connor as the featured vocalist.

Marshall returned for "Heligoland," joining Del Naja and Davidge at Damon Albarn's studio. Four of its tracks emerged first on "Splitting the Atom," which was released in October 2009. The EP's title track, featuring Albarn on keyboards, is propelled by rigid handclaps under vocals by Marshall and Andy, a yin-and-yang pairing. Arriving like midnight fog in a suspense film, "Pray for Rain" featured the voice of TV on the Radio's Tunde Adebimpe, syncopated percussion and what sounded like a bass clarinet; it would serve as the opener to "Heligoland." The two other "Splitting the Atom" tracks were early versions of "Heligoland" final tracks. In both versions of "Psyche," singer Martina Topley-Bird was the centerpiece. "Bulletproof Love" emerged as "Flat of the Blade" on "Heligoland" with the appropriately creepy vocals by Elbow's Guy Garvey pushed to the fore and supported by strings and warm brass.

The full album was issued in early February. Featuring Topley-Bird on vocals, "Babel" was a battleground in which the mellow synths struggled for influence against a fat bass and racing percussion. (The drums won.) Davidge's bass was like a stalker under Andy's quivering vocal on "Girl I Love You," wherein the clang of the cymbal bell was swamped by brass. Albarn sang "Saturday Come Slow," a slow-brewing ballad that wouldn't have sounded out of place on his "Everyday Robots," issued four years later. Chiming keys welcomed the vocal by Mazzy Star's Hope Sandoval on "Paradise Circus."

"Heligoland" spawned several remix EPs and bonus tracks are now available, including "Fatalism," which didn't make it on the original release, but was remixed beautifully by Ryuichi Sakamoto and Yukihiro Takahashi. The album sold well in most countries, but not in the U.S., were it went no higher than 46th place on the Billboard charts. "Paradise Circus" served as the theme song to TV's "Luther," much as "Teardrop" from "Mezzanine" was the opening theme to "House." (Massive Attack is a favorite of filmmakers; their songs have been used about 90 times in movies, TV and video games.)

With "Heligoland," Massive Attack, which started as a DJ and production team, had morphed into a full-fledged band. The album's ingenious tracks reveal the breadth of creativity Del Naja, Marshall and their many contributors had explored in their search for a new way.

Leviathan

Mastodon | *2004*

A classic novel provided inspiration for a new approach to metal.

For its second release, Mastodon chose to record a concept album based in no small part on Herman Melville's "Moby-Dick." On first blush, the 1851 novel seems unusual fare for a heavy-metal recording, but its themes of obsession, revenge, combat, adventure, power and domination suit the genre, as the band proved with "Leviathan."

To be sure, Mastodon is a distinctive heavy-metal group. Drummer Brann Dailor, guitarist Brent Hinds, guitarist Bill Kelliher and bassist Troy Sanders mixed metal sub-genres and added a dose of prog rock and other kinds of complex, power-rich music. Dailor's distinctive playing was influenced by jazz, prog rock and funk. Their music might be called 21st-century metal — that is, a new approach to a genre that at the time was entering its fifth decade as one of rock's most popular forms.

"Leviathan" opened with metal tropes: a guitar statement; frantic percussion as the band folded in; choppy, chugging chords in the mid-range; from-the-belly vocals — all well done with drive and purpose. In "Blood and Thunder," Melville's Captain Ahab addressed the whaling ship Pequod's crew: "When you see the white whale/Break your backs and crack your oars, men, if you wish to prevail.

The album built to speed as twin guitars played in harmony at the end of "Blood and Thunder," then surrendered to the roar of "I Am Ahab," with its blistering dual guitars playing in unison with Sanders' bass. The tempo slowed down with "Seabeast," which threatened as it unfolded. Under the wash of guitars, Dailor was splendid here — in essence, he soloed throughout the song yet never wavered from his responsibility to drive the band. Guitars stung and squealed.

"Iron Tusk," with its allusions to prog rock, was a gory recitation of vicious battles with whales — with a chilling postscript: "Engage monster, wreaking havoc/Assault with all martial rage/Sail on." "Megalodon" zigged and zagged among different time signatures; at one point, the music stopped entirely and a country lick on guitar filled the emptiness until the band returned with fury, pausing only to allow knotty interplay between Dailor and the relentless guitars.

The band veered from the explicit "Moby-Dick" theme with "Naked Burn" and "Aqua Dementia." The former referenced biblical giants and fallen angels, the latter an apocalyptic trial by fire. In the masterful "Naked Burn," the guitars sounded like violins at the opening as well as after a tricky interlude in which Hinds, Kelliher and Sanders pushed Dailor. With Scott Kelley from Neurosis joining in on vocals, "Aqua Dementia" hurdled and brutalized with hardcore guitars. After the chaos subsided, the track concluded with lapping water. That sound bled into the 13-minute suite "Hearts Alive," which opened patiently, but returned with the fiery power echoing an earlier form. It was a startlingly effective, complex marriage of metal and prog rock that served the conclusion of the narrative — the destruction of the Pequod, its crew trapped in a deadly whirlpool: "I can't stand, I can't breathe/Terrified, ghastly cry/Spiraled lives taken down." The album ended with an instrumental ballad featuring acoustic guitars and organs.

Expertly performed, "Leviathan" has the range and scope of an epic tale, which suits its concept. The band toured aggressively behind it, raising their profile considerably as Mastodon became acknowledged as perhaps the greatest metal band of its era. And their "Leviathan" is widely considered to be the best heavy-metal album of the new century.

BLACKsummers'night

Maxwell | *2009*

A return to traditional R&B without sacrificing slinky sensuality

Maxwell waited eight years to release "BLACKsummers'night," his third studio album. Though one of the architectures of the neo-soul movement, Maxwell chose to return with a sound that tilted more toward traditional R&B and soul while retaining the slinky sensuality of his early work. It was as if he pulled the past to the present without acknowledging any current popular trend.

What jumps out from the opening bars of "BLACKsummers'night" is the presence of a band; thus one trend Maxwell skipped was the reliance on synthesized music in pop, hip hop and modern R&B. The core seven-piece group featured a horn section, saxophone, trumpet and trombone, while Chris Dave and Derrick Hodge, young veterans who went on to join Robert Glasper's band, provided drums and bass, respectively. Longtime Maxwell collaborator Hod Davis played guitars.

The communication between Maxwell and the band gave "BLACKsummers'night" a dimension that seemed missing from other mainstream albums of the era. On the ballads "Stop the World" and "Fistful of Tears," the band reacted to Maxwell's vocal performance: when he found a lyric he wanted to emphasize, his bandmates rose up with him. When he eased off to let a note or memory linger, they withdrew too. If a musician seized the suddenly open space, he surrendered it when Maxwell was ready to resume the story. On organ, Shedrick Mitchell seemed particularly intuitive, slipping a pillow under the singer's voice or dashing off a little lick when the opportunity arose.

Born Gerald Maxwell Rivera in Brooklyn, Maxwell played club dates in New York before signing with Columbia when he was 21. His debut, "Maxwell's Urban Hang Suite," was a landmark in the last century's final decade, slipping nicely into the continuum of poignant, romance-laced and quietly sophisticated African-American music. From the beginning, Maxwell was compared favorably to American icons Marvin Gaye, Al Green, Prince and Smokey Robinson.

His 1998 "Embrya" was a bit more free-flowing than its predecessor, with song structure giving way to textured grooves. With "Now," which came out in 2001, Maxwell veered back toward his debut sound. For "BLACKsummers'night," he said he wanted a sound for his new release that was less smooth and more assertive than on his previous discs.

There was no shortage of smooth on the album — Maxwell was as smooth as velvet when the mood required — but the band pushed him to get outside himself. "Cold" sounded like it was recorded live: Maxwell heated up as percussive single notes on guitar and a pattern on the high hat teed up a blast of horns, and Dave responded with an assertive performance. "Fistful of Tears" was a bold heartbreak ballad that permitted the singer to riff on the theme as the staccato music pressed on relentlessly. In "Help Somebody," the piano sounded like a barroom upright; accordingly, Maxwell added a bit of rasp to his voice as he settled in amid a raggedy environment in which bassist Hodges provided the energy.

Though the up- and mid-tempo number gave the album a boost, simmering ballads carried "BLACKsummers'night." The opener, "Bad Habits," floated on Mitchell's quivering chords on organ and fat notes on the bottom by Hodges. An extended outro allowed the horn players to freestyle over the bubbling percussion. Maxwell turned to his quietest side on "Playing Possum," in which he sang in his natural range and in falsetto over David's strummed acoustic guitar. In both instances, Maxwell's performances were just right — gritty when they needed to be, soft and warm when the lyric called for that mood.

With "BLACKsummers'night" Maxwell proved that, despite the eight-year layoff, he'd lost none of his considerable skill. The album met the need for timeless soul music and reconnected listeners to a master of the art form.

The ArchAndroid

Janelle Monáe | *2010*

A funky concept about a machine in love

What to make of a concept album by an artist portraying a heartsick, time-traveling android? Whether the hypothesis is intriguing or off-putting, in the case of "The ArchAndroid" by Janelle Monáe, it works: the music excels and so does she. With her second album, Monáe delivered a surprising and satisfying soul-pop classic.

"The ArchAndroid" is parts two and three of her "Metropolis" that was inspired to a degree by Fritz Lang's extraordinary 1927 sci-fi film. Musically, Monáe drew from many sources, including Michael Jackson, Kid Creole and the Coconuts, OutKast, Prince and Stevie Wonder.

The album opened with "Suite II Overture," a stirring orchestral piece that gave way to "Dance or Die," a slice of Latin-flavored funk in which Monáe rapid-fire rap-sang: "If you see your clone on a street walking by/Keep on running for your life cause only one will survive." Thus, we were thrust into a dystopian society with an android named Cindi Mayweather as our guide. War raged, destruction abounded. A guitar soloed over a blast of horns until "Dance or Die" melded into "Faster," in which Monáe introduced a parallel theme: Cindi, who may be society's savior, is in love — with a human, Anthony Greendown. On the racing track, Monáe flexed the supple timbre of her singing voice. Within the span of its first three songs, "The ArchAndroid" revealed it was to be no ordinary pop experience.

As the story developed, Monáe covered a range of soul and R&B styles. "Locked Inside" profited from a fat bass line.

A cheesy synth ushered in "Sir Greendown," a '50s-style ballad with a modern foundation. "Come Alive" could've come out of the Cab Calloway songbook. "Tightrope," the album's big hit, sounded like a tribute to OutKast, whose Antwan "Big Boi" Patton was featured on the track. "Ladies and gentlemen, the funkiest horn section in Metropolis," Monáe announced, crediting the musicians who gave the track its sizzle.

By the time the first part of the tale ended, several of Monáe's backing musicians had made their marks, suggesting the album was a collaborative effort. Kellindo Parker played most of the lead guitar parts; Wolfmaster Z provided percussion, synths and other instruments; and Roman GianArthur Irvin arranged the voices. Nate "Rocket" Wonder wrote the string charts and conducted the orchestra in addition to playing synthesizers and other keyboards, vibraphone, percussion and more.

As "The ArchAndroid" continued, other resources emerged: after the lush, bittersweet "Suite III Overture," Monáe tapped Stevie Wonder's reading of Rodgers and Hart's "With a Song in My Heart" to enrich "Neon Valley Street." Giving voice to Cindi's ongoing plight, Monáe sang: "We met alone forbidden in the city/ Running fast through time like Tubman and John Henry/…It's such a pity that the city's just a danger zone." Of Montreal's Kevin Barnes wrote "Make the Bus" and his band provided backing support. The duo Deep Cotton gave "57821" a '60s folk vibe. (The number referred to the prison cell in which Greendown is held.) Love and the fight for freedom were concurrent themes: "Sir Greendown told his dear Cindi/Fight like Achilles in Troy/I will show you the ways that I love you/I saved you so you'd save the world.'"

"The ArchAndroid" wrapped up with two extraordinary performances by Monáe and the band: a mid-tempo love ballad "Say You'll Go" and "BaBopByeYa," a dramatic bluesy suite in an action noir film. Monáe sang much of the former accompanied by solo piano; as the ballad faded, "BaBopByeYa" opened with a blast of brass and followed a spoken-word interlude with a moving violin solo by Alexander Page.

"The ArchAndroid" went on to win the Grammy for the Best Contemporary R&B album. In 2013, Monáe released "The Electric Lady," which continued the Cindi saga with "The ArchAndroid" team and guest performances by Erykah Badu, Miguel, Prince, Solange, Esperanza Spalding and others.

As for what happened to Cindi Mayweather and Greendown, the answer can be found by savoring the experience of "The ArchAndroid" from start to end.

The Night

Morphine | *2000*

Four a.m. in the back room of a seedy strip club; a broken neon light sizzles and flickers outside the flophouse across the alley. The scent of cheap bourbon and stale cigarettes hangs around in a pitiless cloud.

That's the ambiance embodied by Morphine, a trio whose music was somber, ironic, witty and monumentally entertaining. And was played by little more than drums, a two-string bass and a baritone saxophone, and sung by the late Mark Sandman, whose

With a canvas limited by choice, Morphine expressed themselves with surprising dexterity.

matter-of-fact, melodic style was the musical equivalent of a gritty Jim Thompson novel.

With a canvas limited by choice, Morphine had but a few ways to express themselves and did so with surprising dexterity on "The Night," their sixth album. Giving rise to an almost palpable mood, drummer Billy Conway and saxophonist Dana Colley listened carefully, and responded, to Sandman's vocals conveying his finely observed tales of love gone wrong, men who know they're bound to lose and events that are doomed to end very, very badly.

Morphine formed in Cambridge, Massachusetts, in 1989 and gained a cult status among students who heard the band on their college radio stations and read about them in the alternative press. The group continued to build its fan base through endless touring and word of mouth; a live album, "Bootleg Detroit," recorded in 1994, gives a sense of how special the trio could be. As the 21st century approached, Morphine was on verge of attaining a plateau that seemed beyond its cool, retro-yet-oddly contemporary sound.

But in July 1999, Sandman suffered a fatal heart attack on stage in Italy. "The Night" was issued after his sudden death. Though it wasn't designed to, it served as both a memorial and a tribute to his gifts as a composer, distinctive bassist and a vocalist whose baritone was perfect for the mood he sought to convey.

On "The Night," the core instrumentation was augmented by discrete piano, organ, strings and percussion; a female choir fit nicely above the backbeat on one tune. Songs were built around Sandman's lyrics, which in turn melded into the commanding, relentless music, forming the perfect marriage of sound and words to create a cohesive result. Sandman's voice often seemed to float from the ether as he narrated yet another dark scene.

Perhaps Morphine's most restrained album, "The Night" contained some of Sandman's best writing, the kind of narratives that insinuated into the subconscious. His lyrics here were noir gems: "If I could only remember the name that's enough for me 'cause names hold the key," he sang in "Souvenir." In "Like A Mirror," he sang drolly: "I'm like a mirror. I'm nothing until you look at me." Great lines kept coming: "You're a bedtime story, one who keeps the curtains closed"; "Ramona and a man do a tango dip, cheek to cheek, hip to hip"; "No, there's nothing too romantic about the way we met/That's not to say it doesn't make a certain sense." How many screenwriters who toiled on noir dramas in the '40s had Sandman's gift for the atmospheric phrase?

Understated and biting, "The Night" encourages investigation of Morphine's full body of work and Sandman's contribution to American rock. The album was, and remains, worthy on its own.

Organik

Niacin | *2005*

There's a sense that the jazz-fusion era ended before the 21st century began. It's a generalization that denies the work of Chick Corea Elektric Band, John McLaughlin and the Fourth Dimension, the late Joe Zawinul's various projects, two early-in-the-century albums by Allan Holdsworth, and the occasional foray into jazz fusion by Christine McBride, among others. There's also the ongoing synthesis of jazz and funk best exemplified by the music of saxophonist Steve Coleman.

Jazz fusion dead? This trio says forcefully, no.

Another great refutation of the "fusion is dead" cry is the music of Niacin, featuring drummer Dennis Chambers, keyboardist John Novello and bassist Billy Sheehan. Their album "Organik" is loaded with startling interpretations of jazz fusion and just about every form of music that informs it, including prog rock, blues and most notably organ-driven jazz. The trio's name is a play on the name of the Hammond B3 electric organ; Niacin is also known as vitamin B3.

While the band members, particularly Novello and Sheehan, cite prog-rock bands like Emerson, Lake and Palmer, early Genesis, King Crimson and Yes as influences, "Organik" was also rooted in electric jazz as conveyed by Corea's Return to Forever and McLaughlin's Mahavishnu Orchestra, among others. "Stumble on the Truth" was jazz blues as a hurdling high-speed train, with all three musicians providing the velocity; midway through the tune, Novello doubled a tricky solo by Sheehan while Chambers seemed to play the spaces in between. "King Kong" swung as Chambers channeled Elvin Jones; late in the performance, Novello switched to acoustic piano, giving the flashy tune another dimension. "Magnetic Mood" began as a jazz blues but, as so often happened with Niacin, there was an sudden, unexpected shift: after Novello soloed beautifully and imaginatively above a groove dug by Chambers and Sheehan, there came a piercing squeal and a blast of notes from a guitar synthesizer. Soon, the wildness receded and Novello returned to the top above the jazz groove.

Meanwhile, the album opened with "Barbarians @ the Gate," which traveled into Frank Zappa territory, then flowed into "Nemesis," which, despite some serious muscling up by Chambers, never lost its feel for first-generation funk. "No Shame" was steely funk with the trio holding tight to the reins. The halting "Hair of the Dog" left its safety zone for a jarring orchestral interlude it abandoned quickly and never revisited, thus adding a dab of wit to a trick out of ELP's bag.

One of the joys of Niacin and "Organik" was how little the band cared about preserving artificial barriers among different genres of electric music. In "Club Soda," Sheehan tossed in a walking bass line under Novello's workout that straddled jazz fusion and prog rock. "4'5 3" began as power rock with a knotty head, but soon found and stayed with a jazz groove before sliding into prog rock. Novello nodded to early Stevie Wonder synth lines in "Clean House" before switching to the B3 sound that set up a brief, rubbery Sheehan solo.

Now and then, "Organik" careened into overdrive. Propelled by Sheehan, "Blisterine" kicked off like a Primus track, then charged into raw jazz fusion featuring a bazillion notes by Novello and Sheehan at death-defying speed. A lot happened, much of it amazing, but to what end? And yet, as Rush fans may attest, sometimes it's a treat to see how far a band can go with its chops.

Niacin regrouped in 2013 for "Krush," another varied, high-octane exercise. Given the members' schedules, it may be a while before they reunite again. In the meanwhile, there's "Organik," the best of the group's demonstration in the studio of the vitality remaining in jazz fusion, especially when it grabs from parallel forms.

Channel Orange

Frank Ocean | *2012*

Balancing
fantasy and
the reality
of hard times

Though his reputation had gathered momentum in the world of hip hop and urban music, Frank Ocean was almost a stranger to mainstream music fans when he released his debut solo album "Channel Orange." The disc was an immediate and well-deserved success for its take on contemporary R&B and its lyrical conten.

Born Christopher Edwin Breaux in Long Beach, California, Ocean moved as a child with his family to New Orleans. After high school, he enrolled at the University of New Orleans, but Hurricane Katrina drove him west to Los Angeles, where he began to sell his compositions. Justin Bieber, Brandy and John Legend were among the vocalists who introduced Ocean songs.

Ocean joined the rap collective Odd Future featuring Tyler, The Creator and Earl Sweatshirt, among others. In 2011, he released "Nostalgia, Ultra," a free mixtape that showcased his sweet, smooth voice; gift for wordplay and narrative storytelling; sensitive approach to production; and wide-ranging taste in popular music.

After co-writing and singing on two tracks on "Watch the Throne," the album by Jay Z and Kanye West, he released "Channel Orange."

The lead single, "Thinkin' about You," was released three months before the full album arrived. It was a pleasing harbinger: a mellow blend of R&B and hip-hop rhythms for a story that was full of sorrow expressed with wit and prickly cynicism. It was nominated for a Grammy for Record of the Year. Two other singles arrived before the full album: "Pyramids," an up-tempo number with assertive percussion pushed by a synth bass; and the jazzy "Sweet Life" with bubbling keyboards and electric bass. In the former, Ocean used the legend of Cleopatra as metaphor for the plight of black women in America; in the latter, written with Pharrell Williams, he declared he was enjoying his stay in southern California. Throughout the album, Ocean balanced a sense of fantasy about life and love with observations on hard times that rebuked his view of a dream world.

Two weeks before the release of "Channel Orange," Ocean announced his first true love was a young man he'd met four years earlier. "We spent that summer, and the summer after, together...(When) we were together, time would glide. By the time I realized I was in love, it was malignant. It was hopeless," Ocean wrote, adding, "I don't have any secrets I need kept anymore...I feel like a free man."

Before "Channel Orange" presented Ocean as a singer-composer at the crossroads of contemporary and traditional soul, funk, R&B and hip hop — influenced by all, but prison of none. "Lost" and "Sierra Leone" tapped the tradition of African-American music, but infused it with a distinctive perspective and a sparse approach to arrangements. With Earl Sweatshirt on hand to rap and a riff from Elton John's "Bennie and the Jets" providing the springboard, "Super Rich Kids" took a hard look at wealthy young people with "nothing but loose ends...(and) fake friends." Ocean conveyed the viewpoint of one of the spoiled boys, who has a moment of clarity before tragedy strikes.

"Channel Orange" sold well and resulted in international acclaim for Ocean from fans and critics. He toured widely, headlined at Lollapalooza, and tossed in songs by Beyoncé, Prince and Sade in his performances. He's yet to issue a follow-up album, but "Channel Orange" continues to fill the void by seeming to get better in the passage of time. It's a special recording.

Stankonia

OutKast | *2000*

Hip hop, rap and R&B from the place from which all things funky come

"Stankonia" marked a change in style for André Benjamin and Antwan Patton, known as André 3000 and Big Boi, respectively. On their prior three albums, the duo hinted at a broad view of hip hop and rap, mixing in down-tempo numbers and Spartan tracks riding on slinky but secure foundations. Gospel and neo-soul informed some songs; humorous tunes and pointed political commentary were delivered side-by-side. Among other songs, "13th Floor/ Growing Old," a penetrating ballad on the album "ATLiens" revealed their independence from the era's standards for rap and hip hop music.

Aware that a national, cross-genre audience was in reach, Outkast focused their diverse approach to popular music across the span of "Stankonia" — "the place from which all funky things come," according to the narrator on the opening track — and did so without dulling their style. They delivered a tight, unified sound — no small task, considering that André 3000 and Big Boi had a different vision of how they should communicate. At least part of the time, they had their eye on commercial success.

Flawless backing tracks gave the album its sense of unity, despite tapping into varying forms of popular music. "B.O.B." — in many ways, the duo's philosophy for "Stankonia" condensed in a song — was built on a platform of frantic drum-and-bass cleaved by David Whild Brown's searing guitar solo. "Humble Mumble" rode on a relentless bubbling percussion track, and "Toilet Tisha" featured a popping bass and a stinging guitar. The infectious "Spaghetti Junction" floated over sampled horns and a flute, and the duo's first pop hit "Ms. Jackson," written on acoustic guitar by André 3000, sampled the Brothers Johnson, Shuggie Otis and Wagner's wedding march; Cameo's Aaron Mills played bass, giving the track its alluring bounce.

Throughout "Stankonia," OutKast commented on social injustice. "Xplosion" addressed the sense of hopelessness among the underclass: "We just can't be amazed even if you pull the pin from your hand grenade." In several tunes, fellow rappers were criticized for flaunting the high life while others continued to suffer. "You gettin' on my nerves/Well, I'm getting' on your case/ Consider your surroundings or you leave without a trace" was how André 3000 put it in "Red Velvet." "Toilet Tisha" was a terrifying tale of how a 14-year-old pregnant girl addressed her dilemma.

André 3000 and Big Boi brought soul crooning into their mix. "So Fresh, So Clean" drew inspiration from R&B singer Joe Simon, and a Curtis May-field-like vocal was at the heart of "Slum Beautiful." Yet rap dominated their sound. "Snappin' & Trappin'" was in-your-face rap and toasting above a staccato drum. In "Humble Mumble," which features Erykah Badu, rap is delivered in two-part harmony.

"Stankonia" earned OutKast two Grammys: one for Best Rap Album, the other for Best Rap Performance by a Duo for "Ms. Jackson." The hit double album "Speakerboxxx/The Love Below" — essentially a solo album each by Benjamin and Patton in one package — and the singles "Hey Ya!" and "The Way You Move" expanded the duo's fan based far beyond hip hop and rap. They made a film, "Idlewild," for which they provided the soundtrack. Both men pursued careers in acting; Benjamin played Jimi Hendrix in the film "All Is by My Side." After a hiatus, Outkast reunited in 2014 for a 25th anniversary tour.

In many ways, "Stankonia" served as the bridge to their huge commercial success from the duo's early days in which they were creating a distinctive voice as pioneers of Southern-style hip hop and rap. The best of what came before and nods to what would follow can be found on the 2000 release.

Raising Sand

Robert Plant and Alison Krauss | *2007*

Leaving behind past achievements to add a new dimension to exemplary careers

Long before they formed their duo to record "Raising Sand," Alison Krauss and Robert Plant had extraordinary reputations in their respective music fields. Krauss recorded her first solo as a teen and by the time she turned 21, was a member of the Grand Ole Opry and winner of two Grammys for Best Bluegrass Album. (She's won 25 additional Grammys.) As a solo artist and with her band Union Station, she moved on occasion beyond bluegrass, country and folk, covering rock and pop tunes with characteristic beauty and deceptive ease.

As for Plant, it's common knowledge that he achieved mega-stardom as a singer and composer with Led Zeppelin, which disbanded in '80. But in the years prior to his alliance with Krauss, he recorded eight solo albums, two others with Zeppelin mate Jimmy Page, and an EP of early R&B and rock & roll. Perhaps more so than any of his contemporaries, Plant placed his former band in a proper context: an important part of, but by no means the entirety, of his legacy; and a remnant of a past life that could imprison him if he didn't resist.

T-Bone Burnett produced "Raising Sand" and was credited with presenting Krauss and Plant with a catalogue of songs to suit their styles. This might've been so, though the singers were likely to have to known the compositions by Kathleen Brennan and Tom Waits, Gene Clark, the Everly Brothers, Mel Tillis, Allen Toussaint and Townes Van Zandt that they covered on the album. Little Milton's "Let Your Loss Be Your Lesson" was the kind of

R&B gem Plant prized, as was "Rich Woman," the album opener that Li'l Millet and His Creoles cut in 1955.

But there was no doubt that Burnett applied a guiding hand and pulled together the extraordinary musicians who supported Krauss and Plant. Drummer Jay Bellerose and bassist Dennis Crouch were the supple spine of the rhythm section. Marc Ribot and Greg Leisz, on guitar and pedal steel, respectively, added color and character to the surroundings, which drew in large part from rockabilly and an off-kilter take on folk.

Krauss and Plant were splendid. The Brennan-Waits tune "Trampled Rose" was given a spooky reading by Krauss in a sparse environment, and her reserved performance on Clark's country ballad "Through the Morning, Through the Night" was perfect. She let loose on the Little Milton tune, which profits from a tasty Ribot solo. Plant took the lead on Toussaint's "Fortune Teller" and toyed with the slinky rhythm around him. On Van Zandt's "Nothin'," the most radically reimagined track on the disc, he sang with deliberation amid a noisy tumult.

The vocal duets provided the most delightful moments on "Raising Sand." Krauss and Plant drew from the Everlys kind of close harmonies for the easy rocking "Rich Woman" and "Gone, Gone, Gone" and Doc Watson's misty-mountain ballad "Your Long Journey." They took a different approach to harmony on the reinvented "Please Read the Letter" and Rowland Salley's "Killing the Blues," and it worked just as well. Conveying a natural simpatico that went behind two highly skilled pros doing their jobs, Krauss and Plant sounded like they enjoyed the work and knew it was going well.

Krauss and Plant toured behind the album, adding Zeppelin tunes into the mix, including Memphis Minnie's "When the Levee Breaks," which they returned to its country-blues roots. "Raising Sand" went on to win the Grammy for Album of the Year. The duo reunited to write and record a follow-up, but weren't satisfied with the early results. Plant formed the Band of Joy with Patty Griffin as his vocal partner. In 2011, Krauss reunited with Union Station for "Paper Airplane," a lovely, melancholy album that embraced bluegrass, folk and country in an immaculate setting.

In making "Raising Sand," an album that's easygoing, witty and a little bit mischievous, Krauss and Plant left behind past achievements and came together as peers to add a new dimension to their acclaimed and already non-traditional careers.

Kid A

Radiohead | *2000*

A revolution
born out of
the need
to change
everything

"Kid A" was born out of the band's own excellence and the radical revolution in the way modern music was conceived and created.

Three years earlier, Radiohead issued a masterpiece, "OK Computer," an album of anthemic ballads and textured guitar-oriented rock. It was a massive hit, raising the group's profile to household-name status and selling more than eight million copies worldwide. Radiohead clones emerged, devaluing the group's sound. Thus had they continued on the same path, they would've been competing with themselves. Having already made in "OK Computer" an album that felt like the pinnacle of commercial alt-rock, moving to a new form of expression made great sense.

"We felt we had to change everything," said Colin Greenwood, the band's bassist. With "Kid A," the quintet, then in its 15th year, redirected contemporary rock and pop.

The close-knit group debated and strategized. Singer and composer Thom Yorke expressed a particular disillusionment with rock and was feeling the liberating influence of electronic music, as had his colleagues. When the band reconvened to write and record, guitars were nudged aside as synthesized sounds became a focus. The classically trained Jonny Greenwood incorporated the ondes Martenot, an early electronic instrument, into the group sound. Self-generated samples and others found elsewhere contributed to the new direction. The band cut almost 30 songs as it moved toward what became "Kid A."

As if to symbolize how the album would differ from its predecessors in the Radiohead catalogue, it began with "Everything in its Right Place," a song build on Yorke's dissembled and manipulated voice, synthesized keyboards and electronic percussion. Not only are there no guitars, but there is no lyrical narrative either: Yorke sings phrases that hint at imagery. Similarly, there is no narrative in the title track, which features chiming keyboard and bouncing bottom tones until drummer Phil Selway enters with a skittish pattern. The percussion dissolves as orchestral swells emerge.

Several tunes hinted at the classic Radiohead sound. An acoustic guitar, electric bass and Yorke's voice introduced "How to Disappear Completely," which expanded with grand, sweeping Messiaen-influenced strings and, deep in the distance, free brass. "The National Anthem" kicked off as a straight-ahead rock tune with Yorke playing a repeating bass pattern, but soon a frenzied eight-piece free-jazz horn ensemble entered. Coming to the fore after the languid instrumental "Treefingers," "Optimistic" rose from a chugging guitar that was soon surrounded by a dense wall of sound from which arise alternating guitar and bass lines before fading out with a bit of funk. Swirling synthesized orchestral sounds provided the underpinning for "Motion Picture Soundtrack."

With "Idioteque," the band revealed some of the roots of their affection for electronica. Jonny Greenwood had created a long electronic piece that drew from a mid-'70s experimental work by Paul Lanksy. He gave it to Yorke, who found within it a segment that he edited into the foundation for the song, which was characterized by repeating and unwavering sparks of percussion. As it faded, Selway's drumming introduces "Morning Bell" in which Yorke sang: "Howling down the chimney, release me, release me/I wanted to tell you but you never listened. You never understand" — a lyric that may address personal turmoil, romantic discord or his anticipation of a reaction to the band's new direction. Darting tones and rounded bass notes formed the liquid support for his vocal.

"Kid A" is widely considered to be the best album of the 21st century. "Amnesiac," released a little more than a year later, comprises tracks recorded during the so-called "Kid A" sessions and, if less startling, is just as intriguing.

But with "Kid A," Radiohead created a new path for contemporary musicians. In doing so, it became, in the recording studio, the most important rock band since the Beatles.

Ecstasy

Lou Reed | *2000*

Groping to
understand
the meaning
and value
of love

A 77-minute contemplation on personal re-
lationships, Lou Reed's "Ecstasy," released in
2000, revealed a state of mind that questioned
his fundamental expectations of love, intimacy and marriage. Distrust and deception de-
fined them on Reed's 18th solo album.

In "Paranoia in the Key of E," love was
compared to diseases, though Reed fret-
ted as he saw it dribbling to an end: "Who
thought this could happen to us when we
first went to bed." As so often in his lyr-
ics, everyday references brought his lines to life: "I know I
shouldn't have had someone else in our bed.../Who would
think you'd find a bobby pin," he wrote in "Mad." Anger ex-
poses misogyny in "Baton Rouge": "Well, I once had a car/
Lost it in a divorce/The judge was a woman, of course."

At times on the album, Reed believed in love and wanted it to work: "Maybe you and I could fall in love/Regain
the spirit we once had/You'd let me hold you..." In "Turning
Time Around," a conversation between lovers, a question is
posed: "What do you call love?" A reply: "I'd call love 'time'...
There's never enough time to hold love in your grasp...And
time is what you never have enough of."

Reed's musical career had enjoyed a renaissance in the
prior decade. With John Cale, he released "Songs for Drel-
la," a collection about Andy Warhol that rises above tribute
into the realm of a new form of biography. Then came Reed's
masterpiece, "Magic and Loss," in which he contemplated

how the living must endure the death of loved ones and try to find equilibrium in the aftermath. For his 1996 album, "Set the Twilight Reeling," Reed put together the rhythm section that would contribute to "Ecstasy" as well: Fernando Saunders on bass and Thunder Smith on drums. A lovely, laidback in-concert album, "Perfect Day: Live in London," followed in '98.

For "Ecstasy," Reed brought back Mike Rathke, who played guitar on some of his earlier projects, and added cellist Jane Scarpatoni, Paul Shapiro and Doug Wieselman on saxophones, and Steven Bernstein on trumpet. Reed's wife, Laurie Anderson, played electric violin on three tracks, providing the lovely centerpiece for the instrumental "Rouge."

Captured by Reed and co-producer Hal Willner, the band's meticulous performance put Reed's voice and guitar in clear relief, as Saunders' fretless bass rumbled on the bottom. The horns added a touch of soul (though not always with warmth), as did a choir that slid behind Reed in "Modern Dance." Most tracks crackled with the familiar traits of Reed's school of rock — harsh and as lean as a knife's blade — but several veered onto new, pleasing turf. "Tatters" drew its inspiration from '50s street-corner music while "Baton Rouge" was a classic folk ballad with Rathke's acoustic guitar at its core. Featuring a Saunders solo in the upper register, the title track swung like a samba. "Turning Time Around" was a slow-motion country stroll, and "Rock Minuet" was indeed a minuet, albeit a nasty one, featuring Scarpatoni's not-so-sweet cello. An 18-minute tightly controlled guitar orgy, "Like A Possum" was a bittersweet diatribe built on sordid imagery.

"Ecstasy" didn't sell well; in fact, only Reed's 1972 solo debut did as poorly on the Billboard charts. But it's a powerful and expressive work, rich with insight and character, as Reed groped and stumbled toward understanding the meaning and value of love, all in a diverse and satisfying musical environment.

Chamber Music

Ballaké Sissoko & Vincent Ségal | *2008*

BALLAKÉ SISSOKO
VINCENT SEGAL

CHAMBER MUSIC

The music was a true fusion, the emergence of another third way.

Ballaké Sissoko, a kora player from Mali, and Vincent Ségal, a classically trained cellist from France, played first in Ségal's flat in Paris for several years before introducing their collaboration to the world. Their resulting debut recording, "Chamber Music," was a masterpiece of cross-cultural integration and communication.

In many ways, the partnership wasn't as unlikely as it seemed. Sissoko, a renowned musician at home who worked with the legendary kora player Toumani Diabaté, was experienced at multiethnic enterprises: he had already played with Taj Mahal and recorded with the Italian pianist Ludovico Einaudi. "I don't look at my music as specifically Malian," said Sissoko when we spoke. "I am a musician who has never taken a traditional approach."

Having studied at the National Conservatory of Music and Dance in Lyon, Ségal was part of the electronica duo Bumcello and had supported Elvis Costello, Cesária Évora, Piers Faccini and others. He was backing Chocolate Genius, aka Marc Anthony Thompson, when he and Sissoko met.

Ségal said Sissoko taught him about syncopation and the groove. Sissoko found in Ségal a sympathetic partner who could coax from his instrument melodies, bass tones and modern rhythms. The duo took their formal compositions — seven by Sissoko, three by Ségal — and played with precision without muting the sense of discovery that no doubt rose through improvisations in Ségal's home. The album was recorded at Salif Keita's studio in Bamako, Mali.

The music was a true fusion, the emergence of another third way. On the opening title track, a template was established quickly: plucked and then bowed, Ségal's cello joined in unison with the stinging raindrop-like notes of Sissoko's kora, and then both musicians took turns soloing with the other easing back to provide appropriate support. In "Oscarine," a bolon, or harp, created a rhythm with which Ségal and Sissoko darted and danced delicately, lulling the listener into the music's trance-like warmth — "hypnotic" is a word that can be applied to almost every moment of "Chamber Music." A balafon — African kin to a xylophone — added new colors to "Houdesti" while "Wo Yé N'gnougobine" and "Ma-Ma FC" permitted the two principals to play rapidly over repeating patterns and percussion. But both Ségal and Sissoko seemed more intent on locking in with the persuasive rhythm.

"Some people think African music is all fast," Ségal told me. "It's a stereotype. You have every kind of music there. With the kora, we can play like baroque music." In several songs, in support of his partner, Ségal issued long, stately lines as if in a more traditional Western string ensemble. Similarly, Sissoko contributed when needed, often with only a few notes, when Ségal took the top line. The music, said Sissoko, "was facilitated by the fact that we both listen well."

"Chamber Music" was an unexpected success, allowing the duo to tour widely in Europe and the U.S. In 2013, Sissoko released "At Peace," which Ségal produced and contributed to, and they toured again. Thus, once again, the unexpected duo displayed their sympathetic approach to collaboration that resulted in the remarkable recording.

Tourist

St Germain | *2000*

From France, electronic dance music that swung

Late in the past century arrived a form of electronic music that drew heavily upon jazz and improvisation. Called Nu Jazz, it featured jazz solos above electronic polyrhythms and deep grooves, and at its best it created an intriguing, satisfying hybrid that challenged the definition of jazz. Among the best Nu Jazz artists was Ludovic Navarre, who recorded under the name St Germain. His "Tourist," issued in 2000, was a swinging, often delightful illustration of how exhilarating Nu Jazz could be.

A native of the Paris suburb of Saint Germain-en-Laye, Navarre began his career in music as a DJ, mixing in his sets jazz, blues, R&B, reggae and hip hop with house music coming out of Detroit and Chicago. Computer-savvy, he began creating his own tracks and in the early '90s released some under a variety of aliases. In '93 issued his first single as St Germain. His debut album, "Boulevard," debuted in Europe in '95. (It was released in the U.S. in 2002.) Featuring some of France's finest jazz musicians playing Navarre's compositions, it was a commercial hit. It established Navarre and the St Germain brand, and soon he began to remix tracks by a variety of artists, including Björk.

Navarre withdrew for several years before his return with "Tourist." Its lineup revealed what he'd been doing during his time away: along with French musicians, it included reggae guitar legend Ernest Ranglin and Senegalese jazz singer and percussionist Idrissa Diop. Navarre's embrace of wider international influences strengthened his writing and production, and resulted in an album that was more assertive than its predecessor.

Though "Tourist" is rich with synthesizer-generated percussion and samples, what makes it is the interplay between man and machine. "So Flute" sprang from the breathy, freewheeling flute of Edouard Labor and percolating Latin percussion by Edmundo Carneiro. A gospel organ kicked off the bluesy, mid-tempo "Land of..." which featured twin saxophones and Pascal Ohsé on trumpet. Destrez soloed over a relentless disco beat and sizzling cymbals in "Pont des Arts." "Montego Spleen" was cool jazz-meets-reggae with Ranglin's guitar as its centerpiece.

Navarre used samples wisely. "Sure Thing" opened with a riff John Lee Hooker played on the soundtrack to the film "The Hot Spot." "Rose Rouge" married a loop culled from Dave Brubeck's "Take Five" to a few words spoken by Marlena Shaw on a live version of "Women of the Ghetto" to form the bubbling platform under Ohsé's solos on muted trumpet and Labor on tenor sax. Be they entirely original or sample-based, the St Germain tracks were fluid, enticing and erased the boundary line that stood between some modern musical forms.

After its release, Navarre and group toured behind "Tourist," which sold more than two million copies worldwide. But when the run of concerts ended in the summer of 2002, Navarre disappeared. He re-emerged in late 2015 with a self-titled album that married electronic grooves and the music of Bali. "Tourist" remains a joyous recording that illustrates what can be achieved when a love of jazz and a passion for electronic rhythms travel together to make something new — or in this case Nu.

Is This It

The Strokes | *2001*

THE STROKES IS THIS IT

A proudly retro sound for takes of ennui and discontent

The debut album by the Strokes, "Is This It" was direct, compact and so indifferent its own quality that it wasn't until it ended that its impact registered. Not only did it announce the arrival of a new band of great promise, it reaffirmed that stripped-down indie rock delivered with insouciance retained its appeal.

"Is This It" was proudly retro: singer Julian Casablancas is reported to have said the group wanted their debut to sound like "a band from the past that took a time trip into the future to make their record." Their most apparent influences were the music of the Velvet Underground and, a tad less so, the Ramones, New York bands whose glory days came several decades earlier.

Casablancas, Nikolai Fraiture, Albert Hammond Jr., Fabrizio Moretti and Nick Valensi formed the Strokes in New York and they cut their teeth in Lower East Side clubs. Though the quintet may have struggled in its earliest days, they were, to a degree, children of privilege: Casablancas, Moretti and Valensi met at a posh Manhattan prep school; Fraiture and Casablancas attended together the Lycée Français de New York; and Casablancas and Hammond became friends at a boarding school in Switzerland. Hammond's father Albert had a hit in '72 with "It Never Rains in Southern California" and co-wrote, among other songs, the Hollies' "The Air That I Breathe" and "To All the Girls I've Loved Before," popularized by Julio Iglesias and Willie Nelson.

For all its glory, "Is This It" got off to a dull start with the title track, a lifeless sing-along, but things picked up with "The Modern Age" and "Barely Legal," virtual Velvets tributes that were expertly delivered in a deliberately lo-fi environment with Casablancas channeling young Lou Reed as he sang breathlessly. "Soma" was jangly punk marked by Moretti's straight-ahead drumming, Fraiture's insistent bass and choppy guitars played by Hammond and Valensi. The arrangements were simple but effective: if rock can be sloppy and tight, it was on the first four tracks of "Is This It." Intentionally so, by the way: with "Trying Your Luck," the album's penultimate track, the band demonstrated the instrumental capabilities it concealed previously.

Continuing their tales of the ennui and lowercase traumas of urban youth, the Strokes shifted away from grit and into New Wave mode on "Someday," "Last Nite" and "Alone, Together." While the first two tracks were successful singles for the quintet, "Alone, Together" featured the most energetic performances on the disc including a frantic guitar solo by Valensi and hooky lyrics delivered by Casablancas. In "When It Started," the guitars cleared a lane for Valensi to flit in the mid-range.

In "Hard to Explain," the band played with a drive and focus worthy of the Ramones, with Fraiture pumping away on the bottom and the guitars locking in with Moretti's high hat. It was the group's debut single and it represented them at their best, as Casablancas veered away from his predecessors to establish his own effective style in which urgency and indifference collide in the voice of a young man who was clearly a bit of a wiseass.

"Is This It" did everything a debut album is supposed to. It launched the band with a top seller in the Australia, France, U.K., on the Scandinavian Peninsula and at home. Some critics, in a wild overreach, named it the Best Album of the 2000s. Casablancas and Hammond became celebrities noted for their fashion sense as well as their music. The Strokes have since released four more albums and, after a three-year hiatus, resumed touring in 2014. "Is This It" is a solid, enjoyable recording that serves to pull the past forward and re-energize an old sound so it's fresh, if not quite new.

Have You Ever Been…

Turtle Island Quartet | *2010*

Paying
homage to
an American
treasure as
guitarist and
composer

"Have Your Ever Been…" is Turtle Island Quartet's tribute to the music of Jimi Hendrix. The string quartet's leader, David Balakrishnan, saw Hendrix in concert and, as if on a mission, long sought to adapt the guitarist's music to a classical setting. Hendrix, said Balakrishnan, was a true American genius, not only as a guitar player but as a composer.

Along with Jeremy Kittel on viola, Mark Summer on cello and Mads Tolling on violin, Balakrishnan reimagined eight songs associated with Hendrix including covers like "Hey Joe" and "All Along the Watchtower." "Have You Ever Been…" also featured an original Balakrishnan four-part suite "Tree of Life," a tribute to Charles Darwin; and John McLaughlin's "To Bop Or Not To Be." By juxtaposing Hendrix's works with those compositions, Turtle Island Quartet suggested Hendrix was a kindred spirit to an evolutionary figure in the history of music for electric guitar and a modern-jazz giant.

Turtle Island Quartet was formed in 1985 and since their earliest days envisioned a different sort of repertoire, with an emphasis on jazz. They've reworked and performed compositions by Dave Brubeck, Chick Corea, Miles Davis and Thelonious Monk, among others, and in 2007 released "A Love Supreme: The Legacy of John Coltrane." They first tackled Hendrix with a rendition of his "Gypsy Eyes" on their "Who Do We Think We Are" album, released in 1994. (The version of "Gypsy Eyes" on "Have You Ever Been…"

features jazz vibraphonist Stefon Harris.)

But Hendrix's influence has been with them since their first recording. On the group's eponymous debut album, issued in 1988, Mr. Balakrishnan opened his "Balopadem" suite with the same dominant chord that Hendrix used in his compositions to add tension and color to his blues — it's featured in "Purple Haze," for example. Musicians today refer to it as the "Hendrix chord."

On "Have You Ever Been…" the quartet drove toward the heart of Hendrix's writing and playing by capturing his assertiveness and emotion. Yet the group's performance wasn't subservient: their personalities in their playing were a governing feature of the disc. In "Little Wing," Summer, in a solo performance that was part transcription and part interpretation, not only quoted Hendrix, who overdubbed several guitars on the original track, but also referenced the original bass and percussion parts. The quartet's version of "Voodoo Child (Slight Return)" included the waka-chucka sound Hendrix used to kick off the performance, and the violins played the arpeggios the guitarist tossed in while he sang the melody. Their "House Burning Down" began as dramatically as the original with Balakrishnan giving it a bit of gypsy flair, and then swung more so than the original; Hendrix's flashy ending to the song, full of feedback and studio trickery, was transformed as well.

Since the Hendrix tribute, Turtle Island Quartet released in 2014 "Confetti Man," which included compositions by jazz composers John Carisi, Paquito D'Rivera, Bob Mintzer, Bud Powell and Wayne Shorter, as well as new Balakrishnan pieces. Kittel and Tolling have moved on, and have been succeeded by Mateusz Smoczyński and Benjamin von Gutzeit. With "Have You Ever Been…" the quartet honored Hendrix with their enormous skills and passion for inventiveness.

Who Is Jill Scott?
Words and Sounds, Vol.1

Jill Scott | *2000*

Who Is Jill Scott?

Words And Sounds Vol. 1

The singer-composer arrived with an original, substantial gift.

With her performance, Jill Scott gave the answer to the question she posed in the subtitle of "Who is Jill Scott? Words and Sounds, Vol. 1." Her splendid debut disc revealed a gifted writer, an extraordinary vocalist and a poised, engaging personality who added a distinct element to the world of neo-soul.

Spirited, quietly assertive, jazzy and cool, "Who is Jill Scott?" was a delight from jump to landing. After a brief spoken intro, the album slid into a slice of slinky R&B: "Do You Remember" featured Scott's voice soaring to the peak of its register over a drum pattern and sparse instrumentation. In a statement of who and what the focus would be on the album, she held the light with casual charm and confidence. She also declared that her vision of love is vast — a fantasy and yet anchored in daily experience. "We built castles in the Serengeti/You splashed my face with Nile water … I remember when you got your first pair of sneaks." A repeated theme through the album: love is magnificent, but it's likely to disappoint. In the spoken-word piece "Exclusively," a sniff of a scent and a one-word comment by a supermarket checkout clerk jolted Scott's narrator, who was flush with the afterglow of idyllic love.

But love is worth the risk of pain, Scott insisted. "You got me feeling like a breeze, easy free and lovely and new," she sang over strings in "He Loves Me (Lyzel in E Flat)." And she made it clear that romance is best when both partners enter strong. "So many times I define my pride through somebody else's eyes/Then I looked inside and found my own stride/I found the lasting love for me/If I'm searching for my spirituality passionately, I must begin with me," she stated in "One is the Magic #," in which she was accompanied by a brassy trumpet.

Throughout the album, Scott was the anti-diva. Her character wasn't lost in a misty fairytale. She was making her way through the challenges of daily living, working hard to stay even, trying to hold onto happiness and delighted by the occasional magic moment. One of the most refreshing aspects of the recording is her approachability; another answer question of who is Jill Scott: an artist her listeners could cozy up to.

Raised in North Philadelphia, Scott began her career as a poet and spoken-word artist. Amir "Questlove" Thompson of the Roots brought her into the studio. Shortly thereafter, she joined the Canadian touring company of "Rent." Then came her debut album.

Scott surrounded her words and vocals with a range of modern music, much of it based in down-tempo hip hop. "Love Rain" was a ballad that morphed into a spoken-word piece that floated on hip-hop percussion, but on the remix, the album's hidden track, Mos Def and more assertive drumming altered the mood. Similarly, "A Long Walk" began as a low-key love song, riding on percolating percussion and keyboards, but then Scott raised her voice an octave and a request suddenly seemed a demand.

Working with a variety of co-writers and producers, Scott crafted a collection of evocative songs, many of which scream for re-interpretation by jazz and pop singers. "I Think It's Better," "Try," "Slowly Surely" and the bouncy "It's Love" are a treasure trove for vocalists who want to convey maturity and sensuality.

After "Who is Jill Scott?" she released a live "Experience: Jill Scott 826+," then two more entries to her "Words and Music" series. In 2007 came "Collaborations," an assortment of her performances with George Benson and Al Jarreau, Lupe Fiasco, the Isley Brothers, Mos Def, will.i.am and others. Her 2011 disc "The Light of the Sun" won the Soul Train Award for Best R&B/Soul Album by a female artist. Those recordings provide a definitive answer to "Who is Jill Scott?" — an original and substantial musical talent.

Real Gone

Tom Waits | *2004*

With great songs, pushing experimentation about as far as it could go

Apparently, resting on past laurels held no interest for Tom Waits, who by the time the 21st century arrived was well-established as one of modern music's best songwriters and innovative arrangers who drew from blues, folk, jazz via L.A.'s Central Avenue, and German murder ballads. Such curiosity and encyclopedic knowledge can lead the gifted toward new modes of expression, as it did Waits, much to the delight of his fans who held in similar high regard an appreciation for a variety of forms.

Waits began to move away from traditional musical platforms some 20 years earlier with "Swordfishtrombones." With "Real Gone," his 15th studio album, he pushed his embrace of the experimental about as far as it could go. But the music never lost its bearing nor did it fail to support the narratives crafted by Waits and Kathleen Brennan, his wife and partner as songwriter and producer. Though he brought back musicians he'd used before, including bassist Les Claypool, percussionist Brian Manti, guitarist Marc Ribot and bassist Larry Taylor, Waits deployed them differently in an environment informed at times by what might've been called loose industrial. Casey Waits, a drummer by trade, played more traditional percussion instruments on most tracks, but his turntable scratching added agitation to the mix.

Waits and his ad-hoc band deployed industrial clanking on "Don't Go Into the Barn" as well as "Metropolitan Glide." "Hoist That Rag" bore a Latin groove that Ribot enriched.

On several tunes, the arrangements ran in close parallel to

traditional forms. Steadied by Taylor's upright bass, "How's It Gonna End" invoked the music of the Weimar Republic as well as earlier Waits settings, as did the oily "Dead and Lovely." Fat rock riffs fed the stop-start "Shake It," in which the senior Waits sounded like he was singing through wax paper and a comb. The 10-minute-plus "Sins of My Father" was a loping blues featuring Ribot's banjo and guitar.

Over the years, Waits had discovered ways to utilize his voice as it grew gargly and frayed around the edges. Here, he repeated a high eerie moan as he sang "Trampled Rose" over Ribot's banjo and Taylor's bass. In "Green Grass," he sang in a deep low whisper accompanied by the chop-chop of his guitar chords. One of the joys of Waits' recordings was the spoken-word tracks, and in "Circus," he was supported by a cymbal's sizzle and a Chamberlin, an electronic instrument that produced glass-like chimes.

For the most part, Waits and Brennan avoided overtly political messaging in their songs, but the folk ballad "Day After Tomorrow" was inspired by their discontent with plight of American troops in the Iraq War. A letter home on his birthday by a soldier who is far away, the song was a moving depiction of the juxtaposition of the comforts of family and life back home versus the ready risk of death and the power of disillusion. Its simple setting — guitars, voice, some ambience sounds — was in stark contrast to the arrangements throughout "Real Gone," thus driving focus to the lyrical theme.

With their flair for language, character and situation, Waits and Brennan present a portfolio of quotable lyrics on every album, and "Real Gone" wasn't an exception. Here we met Skinny Bones Jones, Piggy Knowles, Bowlegged Sal, Sing Sing Tommy Shay and Everett Lee, who's "high on potato-and-tulip wine fermented in the muddy rain." Many questions are posed; among them: "Does the light of God blind you or lead the way home?"

Several songs from "Real Gone" were part of the repertoire of Waits' "Glimmer and Doom" tour in 2008 and were included in the subsequent live album of the same name. He didn't release a follow-up studio album to "Real Gone" until 2011's "Bad as Me," which pulled back a bit on the eccentric arrangements. "Real Gone" remains an ingenious recording, full of dark wonder and unexpected delights.

My Beautiful Dark Twisted Fantasy

Kanye West | *2008*

A furious commentary on race, celebrity and consumer culture

After three albums that positioned him as a rap and hip hop superstar, in 2008 Kanye West released "808s & Heartbreak," in which he veered into a form of minimalist electro R&B and sang in a voice cloaked by digital effects. The disc was well received, but its dour mood called into question West's fire and raised speculation that he might pursue a career in pop. Two years later, he swept aside doubt and conjecture with "My Beautiful Dark Twisted Fanta-sy," a powerful recording that astonished with its ambition, breath of influences and expression of mental anguish.

An exercise in collaboration, on "My Beautiful Dark Twisted Fantasy," West was composer and conductor who shared center stage with Drake, Jay Z, Alicia Keys, Kid Cudi, Nicki Minaj, John Legend, Rihanna, Justin Vernon of Bon Iver, and others, each of whom contributed to his grand vision. In his choice of samples, West demonstrated an encyclopedic knowledge of rock and pop, drawing from tracks by Aphex Twin, Black Sabbath, Manu Dibango, Mike Oldfield, Smokey Robinson, Gil-Scott-Heron and the Turtles. Production by Jeff Bhasker, Bink, DJ Frank E, Mike Dean, Emile, West and oth-ers incorporated strings, brass and reeds, and fuzzy electric guitars as well as synthesizers and electronic percussion.

"My Beautiful Dark Twisted Fantasy" opened with a riff by Minaj on Roald Dahl's "Cinderella" from his "Revolting Rhymes" and then featured a melody sung by Teyana Taylor and Vernon, thus suggesting that what followed was a long-form work. Shattering the pop tranquility, West entered with a statement that foreshadowed the narrator's outbursts and the album's overarching theme: "Sorry for the night demons still visit me/The plan was to drink until the pain over/What's worse — the pain or the hangover?"

The clash of melodic pop and furious raps continued through the album. A vocal by Legend over a tender piano (from the Aphex Twin's "Avril 14s") in "Blame Game" was disrupted by a profane rant by Chris Rock. In "Power," which relied on King Crimson's 1969 track "21st Century Schizoid Man," the narrator contemplated suicide. As a choir sang "Jumping out the window, letting everything go," West intoned, "Now this will be a beautiful death."

If there was a song that was "My Beautiful Dark Twisted Fantasy" in microcosm, it was "All of the Lights," which rose from an orchestral interlude as a soul ballad with vocalists Drake, Fergie, Elton John (who also played piano in the outro), Keys, Legend and the Gap Band's Charlie Wilson contributing; Rihanna sang the hook. West's rap set up the story. Finding his lover with another man, the narrator slaps her. The police arrive and he's sent to prison. West delivered the narrator's pleas with raw, affecting power: rife with regret, he wants to save his daughter from the kind of life he suffers.

"My Beautiful Dark Twisted Fantasy" was in part West's commentary on celebrity and consumer culture. Surveying that culture, he aired his grievances, often to an absurd, comic effect. But the album returned repeatedly to a theme of a man full of fury who was isolated and, despite his arrogance, racked with self-doubt: West as thug with a heart of gold. In "Runaway," which grew out a nagging single piano note, he stated: "I'm so gifted at finding what I don't like the most" and "See, I could have me a good girl and still be addicted to them hoodrats."

In the aftermath of "My Beautiful Dark Twisted Fantasy," West pursued the often-ridiculous world of tabloid celebrity and deliberately courted controversy. In public, he can seem at best narcissistic. He's a supreme provocateur. None of these things diminish his achievements. Textured, thematically complex and a coarse, raucous adventure in popular music, "My Beautiful Dark Twisted Fantasy" is a mighty work that reveals a troubled and expressive artist who is much more than he may appear to be.

Yankee Hotel Foxtrot

Wilco | *2002*

yankee hotel foxtrot / wilco

The band altered its lineup and sound — and created a masterpiece.

With "Yankee Hotel Foxtrot," Wilco's Jeff Tweedy went well beyond singer-songwriter conventions by placing traditionally structured compositions in an environment tilting toward the avant-garde. With the newly arrived Glenn Kotche on drums and Jim O'Rourke as de facto producer, the album represented the end of Wilco's initial era — and the beginning of a period in which the band would emerge as the best of its kind.

"Yankee Hotel Foxtrot" had a rocky gestation, both as music and as a product for commerce. Legend has it that the band wasn't comfortable with the work of drummer Ken Coomer, who, along with bassist John Stirratt and multi-instrumentalist Max Johnston, joined Wilco directly after the breakup of Uncle Tupelo, Tweedy's previous band. (Jay Bennett came to the band after Wilco's 1995 debut, "A.M." had been recorded.) In 2000, Tweedy worked with O'Rourke, who had a flair for the experimental, and the two, along with Kotche, formed Loose Fur, giving Tweedy a chance to experience a more progressive setting.

He saw a new future for Wilco. Kotche replaced Coomer and, after the music for "Yankee Hotel Foxtrot" was recorded, Bennett was let go. O'Rourke mixed the album and played a variety of instruments to augment the basic tracks. (The internal squabbling and tension that led to the reconfigured Wilco was captured in the documentary "I Am Trying to Break Your Heart: A Film About Wilco.")

"Yankee Hotel Foxtrot" was ready for release, but turmoil at the band's label, Reprise Records, kept it shelved. In mid-September 2001, tracks began to turn up online; in response, Wilco streamed "Yankee Hotel Foxtrot" on their website. It was released formally in April 2002.

The new music dared to be different from the opening track. "I Am Trying to Break Your Open" meandered as if unfocused until Tweedy's voice and guitar gave it a center that Kotche explored on the kit, and then flirted with cacophony as the heartache story broke apart. It introduced a concept in which many of the songs appeared to be drifting toward a new approach without completely discarding tradition. "Ashes of American Flags" opened as slow-motion rock ballad. "Radio Cure" featured a fingerpicked guitar and a boozy vocal by Tweedy. "Kamera" was misty yet straight-ahead alt-country, albeit with the support of a marimba and the crackle of static. And "War on War" pressed on with driving guitars and Stirratt's pumping bass even as sound effects threatened to swamp the top line.

In several tracks, the band pushed experimentation to the side: in "Jesus, Etc.," the album's strongest track, strings straddled country and pop to give it the only ornamentation it needed. "Heavy Metal Drummer," "I'm the Man Who Loves You" and the lovely, troubling "Poor Places" had the wit and charm of a '60s British pop and rock. (The Beatles seemed a major influence throughout, as did Television and some free-jazz artists.) "I'm the Man Who Loves You" featured a stinging psychedelic garage-band guitar solo and chipper horns.

After Wilco recorded their next album, "A Ghost is Born," which featured newcomer Mikael Jorgensen on keyboards, they added guitarist Nels Cline and multi-instrumentalist Pat Sansone, which allowed them to push further the experimental concept, especially in concert.

With "Yankee Hotel Foxtrot," Tweedy and the band placed the singer-songwriter in a new context. Sonic experimentation and a re-ordering of instrumentation provided a new kind of enriching, clarifying support for the voice and lyric, and it worked wonderfully well. It is the source of what followed from an extraordinary rock group.

Blessed

Lucinda Williams | *2011*

An essential artist explored new subjects with customary excellence.

Having already written and recorded "Car Wheels on a Gravel Road," the '98 album that rocketed her reputation to the heights it deserved, and remarkable songs like "Sweet Old World," "Joy," "Are You Alright?" and others, the songs Williams composed for "Blessed" were her first batch since she married Tom Overby. During a '11 visit, she told me she had been looking forward to writing about something other than unrequited love.

Love and security freed Williams to write about a variety of subjects she hadn't explored. She put the compositions on tape, playing and singing into a recorder at her kitchen table in Studio City, California. In the "Blessed" deluxe package, Williams released the demo recordings as "The Kitchen Tapes."

Williams brought in Don Was to produce the "Blessed" sessions. He wanted keyboard player Rami Jaffee and guitarist Val McCallum on the album while she retained her touring rhythm section of Butch Norton on drums and David Sutton on bass. The core unit was terrific; entirely sympathetic but never reticent: listen to its work on "Born To Be Loved" and "Copenhagen," to name two assertive performances. Williams and Was agreed on what guests to bring in: Matthew Sweet sang along, Greg Leisz played pedal steel and other guitars, and Elvis Costello contributed a few crunchy guitar solos. For the most part, "Blessed" was recorded live in the studio and its unfettered presence was one of its most endearing traits.

As the "Kitchen Tapes" revealed, for all the authority in the ad-hoc band's performance, much of the brilliance of "Blessed" rose from Williams' poignant songs. The opener "Buttercup" was a bitter "get-lost" song about a man who failed her but kept coming around. "Now you want somebody to be your buttercup. Good luck finding your buttercup," she sang in her unmistakable gravelly voice. The mood changed swiftly with the follow-up number "I Don't Know How You're Livin'," a sad kin to "Are You Alright?" in which Williams sings about a missing loved one. An old-fashioned blues stroll, "Born to Be Loved" posited love as a basic human dignity.

The hard-hitting "Seeing Black" was inspired by Vic Chestnutt's Christmas 2009 suicide. Williams' open lyric captured the listener in a phrase: "How did you come up with a day and time?" Her rage and confusion built throughout the song: "Did evil triumph over love? Was it hard to finally pull the plug?" She followed with ballads that helped the listener recover from the stunning blow of "Seeing Black," yet "Soldier's Song" and "Blessed" had a quiet power that was almost comparable. "Sweet Love" was a charmer: "Everything in me and of me is yours forever," she sang. "I would choose never to live a day without you."

The stroll also served as the platform for "Convince Me." The tension in the background made sense: in the song, the narrator wanted to be assured she was loved. "Tell me so I understand/Talk to me and hold my hand," she sang. Just as it appeared she was coming toward believing, she added: "The whole wide world is gonna break apart so, please, please, please convince me." The album concluded with a gorgeous folk ballad "Kiss Like Your Kiss": "There'll never be a winter quite so true/When the sky was painted with gifts/There'll never be a moon so full and blue/There'll never be a kiss like your kiss." Its beauty rounded off an extraordinary collection of songs well played and sung with affecting emotion.

Even before "Blessed," Williams' place in contemporary rock and pop was assured. The 2011 release reaffirmed her status as an essential artist and superb songwriter.

There's More Where That Came From

Lee Ann Womack | *2005*

A powerful singer returns to what she does best

After veering toward pop — with much success, at least early on — Lee Ann Womack returned to country with "There's More Where That Came From," a poignant yet spirited album of songs about love and heartache and about cheating and the inevitable fallout. It was viewed as a comeback by an artist of considerable talent who might have lost her way.

After two albums of traditional heartbreak country in which her sparkling soprano and emotional delivery suggested she might be an heir to Loretta Lynn, Dolly Parton and Tammy Wynette, Womack in 2000 issued "I Hope You Dance," a confident outing that added pop and country-rock to her sound. With its fat electric bass and synthesized strings, the title track, a number-one country hit, crossed over to the pop charts. Her performance of songs by Rodney Crowell, Julie and Buddy Miller, and Bruce Robison foreshadowed the country side of the Americana movement.

The 2002 follow-up, "Something Worth Leaving Behind," failed to spark similar success; though her voice was as compelling as it had always been, the album jumped among styles that pushed Womack far from the environment her audience preferred. She disavowed it. (Taken on its own, it's a much better album than it seems in the context of her career.) Three years later, she released "There's More Where That Came From," which found Womack back doing what she did best: country story-songs in an intimate environment blessed with acoustic guitars and fiddles.

The marriage of Womack's voice and the songs was near-perfect. She began with Odie Blackmon's "I May Hate Myself in the Morning." The opening lyrics foretold the tale: "Ain't it just like one of us to pick up the phone and call after a couple of drinks." Surrounded by dew drops of pedal steel, she built toward a classical country flip of phrase: "I may hate myself in the morning/But I'm gonna love you tonight." An extended outro featured a bittersweet fiddle line by Aubrey Haynie that let the aftermath of the story hang in the air. In the title track, a tawny affair was revealed — "I had forgotten just what love felt like/But in that motel room all my senses came to life" — and the narrator wrestled with guilt and the desire to repeat the experience. Womack conveyed the conflict with deceiving ease. Throughout the recording's 13 tracks, Womack gave her narrators — aimless, hurt but never frail — a hint of mystery: would they bounce back or just drift away?

The album managed the difficult task of going down easy while demanding attention. The natural sunlight in Womack's voice didn't quite disguise the pain radiating from the lyrics. The lovely "The Last Time" was set in an abandoned field that once held a carnival; Womack sang of the man she once brushed off and now missed terribly. "Happiness" wasn't a happy tale despite the clever wordplay. As drums pushed her and a deft piano provided a counterpoint, she sang: "It ain't easy finding happiness." Even an up-tempo number like "When You Get To Me," which balanced a chugging guitar and a sprinkling of mandolin, Womack's voice dripped with loneliness as a man headed on a search she hoped would lead back to her.

"There's More Where That Came From" reached the number-three slot on the Billboard country-album chart. In 2008, Womack returned with "Call Me Crazy," which was nominated for a Grammy for Best Country Album. Then in 2014, she issued a gem, "The Way I'm Livin." Thus, "There's More Where That Came From" was a prophetic title, as Womack continued to deliver spirited country since its release. The album put her back on the track where her best traits shone through.

The Orchard

Lizz Wright | *2008*

Wright's flawless, burnished voice explored blues, folk and pop

Lizz Wright's third studio album, "The Orchard," was the ideal marriage of voice, compositions, arrangements and performances. Producer Craig Street surrounded her with expert musicians, including Oren Bloedow and Chris Bruce on guitars and bass; Kenny Banks, Glenn Patscha and Patrick Warren on keyboards, and Larry Eagles on drums. Calexico's Joey Burns and John Convertino pitched in. Larry Campbell played pedal steel, and Toshi Reagon contributed voice and guitar to many tracks, including six she and Wright composed together.

But make no mistake: it was Wright who put it across. Her flawless, burnished voice was suited perfectly to the album's well-designed blues, folk and pop.

"The Orchard" conveyed a conflict that unraveled as the music unfolded: Wright was a stately presence, formal and controlled, and yet the songs drove her to raw emotion. Without losing her poise, she communicated her feelings, leaning on key lyrics and sustaining notes to draw the listener to the emotion of the tale. No wild flights of melisma here; Wright knew how to use her voice to expose the essence of the song. She did so with subtle yet unmistakable power.

The album opens with three songs that display its range; the first two were written by Wright and Reagon: "Coming Home" is a bluesy folk ballad built on the ringing of an acoustic guitar supported by a whistling organ while "My

Heart" has the snap of funk and gospel. On Ike Turner's "I Idolize You," sung originally by Tina Turner way back in 1961, Wright sands off the edges and turns it into a simmering blues number. Later in the album, Wright covered Led Zeppelin's "Thank You," recasting it as a spry, somewhat bittersweet folk tune that was heated by brass at its peak.

"Hey Mann" was originally recorded by Sweet Honey in the Rock, an a cappella ensemble founded by Bernice Johnson Reagon, Toshi's mom, who composed the love song. Wright turned in a reading so powerful it threatened to overshadow the remainder of "The Orchard." In voice that balanced pride and surrender, Wright sang: "How did you get in here? I don't remember letting you in…You're in my heart without consent." She added: "I've lost the battle and I'm quite well pleased." Campbell's pedal steel gave the arrangement a hint of country.

With Wright in the spotlight, the environment shifted around her. The gospel blues "When I Fall" rode on a single electric guitar supported by a steady thwack on a snare drum. "Leave Me Standing Alone" bounced along with a funky bite. "This Is" and "Another Angel" featured finger-picked acoustic guitars, as did "Speak Your Heart," to which Marc Anthony Thompson contributed as a vocalist. A cello played by Burns, and Campbell's mandolin, sweetened the environment of the stirring ballad "Song for Mia."

The album failed to receive the recognition it deserved, and Wright has yet to be placed firmly in the class in which she belongs. But with "The Orchard" she issued an album worthy of Abbey Lincoln, Odetta, Cassandra Wilson and other vocalists who owned any song they chose to sing. At the same time, it demonstrated fully Wright's distinctive talents while suggesting there is more to come.

Made in the USA
San Bernardino, CA
11 November 2015